FOCUS

*Rethinking the Meaning
of Our Evangelism*

FOCUS
Rethinking the Meaning of Our Evangelism

Malcolm Boyd

Foreword by The Rt. Rev. Frederick H. Borsch

MOREHOUSE PUBLISHING

Copyright © 1960, 2002 Malcolm Boyd

Morehouse Publishing
P.O. Box 1321
Harrisburg, PA 17105

Morehouse Publishing is a division of the Morehouse Group.

Design by Corey Kent

Library of Congress Cataloging-in-Publication Data

Boyd, Malcolm, 1923–
    Focus : rethinking the meaning of our evangelism /
Malcolm Boyd ; foreword by Frederick H. Borsch.
        p.   cm. — (Library of Episcopalian classics)
    Originally published: New York : Morehouse-Barlow Co.,
    1960.
    Includes bibliographical references.
    ISBN 0-8192-1903-7
    1. Evangelistic work—Episcopal Church. 2. Episcopal
Church—Doctrines. I. Title. II. Series.
BV3790 .B62 2002
269'.2—dc21
                                                2001041050

Printed in the United States of America

01 02 03 04 05 06 07 08 09   10 9 8 7 6 5 4 3 2 1

Contents

Foreword

Dinner parties and weddings, farms and vineyards, sowing and reaping, masters and servants, parents and children, sheep and goats, treasure and money, law courts, fish, birds, bread and seeds: they are all featured in Jesus' stories about how the kingdom of God—God's ways—are already part of life.

This is the good news, and the demanding, challenging news, that Jesus proclaims and then enacts in his life and ministry. All kinds of people are invited to participate—men, women, and children, well-to-do and poor, the good and the bad; although the righteous may have to change some of their ideas about being good if they want to enter fully in and not try to keep others out.

Jesus' invitation includes everyone and comes amid everyday circumstances and concerns. This inclusion is also at the heart of Malcolm Boyd's invitation to share the good and challenging news of God's ways. It is, he tells us, what evangelism—sharing good news—is all about.

Those who have used Malcolm Boyd's wonderfully popular *Are You Running with Me, Jesus?* and *The Prayers of Malcolm Boyd* will already know this. Prayers are about what happens to each of us in everyday life. This is true of the faithful sharing of the good news, as well. There are not two worlds—one for religious faith and another for everyday matters and concerns. God's care is the context of all things; Malcolm Boyd's interest in evangelism involves business, the arts and media, science, and politics. He includes church, but that is because church and faithful living are meant to be involved in business, the arts and media, science and politics as well. Faithful Christian living and witness means full participation in the beauty and wonder of life, but also its tough and hard places—the heartbreak and passion of our world.

Malcolm Boyd sees the challenge of racism as an important illustration of how this witness for evangelism is made. Because the gospel is about God's love for all persons, only a church that is struggling fully to embody this invitation in its own community and in the world can make a faithful witness. Indeed, as he points out, the opposite is also true. Christians can do non-evangelism by saying one thing but doing another.

Just as the challenge to live out evangelism includes the whole world and all people, it also involves the whole person. It won't do to try to love and serve God and to love one's neighbor only with one's emotions or just with the intellect. Faithful witness and evangelism mean loving and sharing with heart and mind, soul and strength. Such a committed witness is, of course, a great undertaking and adventure—as it is meant to be.

The response to this challenge might sound like a lot of action and activity, but Malcolm Boyd also knows the vital role of prayer. Moreover, he knows how significant attentiveness and good listening can be for evangelism. One who truly wishes to share with others listens to their stories. One hears their hopes and fears, their joys, worries, and longings. One listens for what they find missing in their lives and then is prepared to offer the hope and invitation of God's ways in Jesus. For the most part, those with whom one listens and shares faith will not be strangers, but friends and neighbors, family members and coworkers who may be waiting for the invitation.

Malcolm Boyd first penned these insights and stories about evangelism some forty years ago. They remain, however, as fresh as the understanding that evangelism includes the whole world, the full person, and all people. It is here that the spirit of God, best known to Christians through Jesus, is present to enliven and confirm the witness to evangelism that is at the heart of Christian faith and living.

Frederick H. Borsch
Bishop of Los Angeles
June 4, 2001

I. Who, What, When, Where, How?

Almighty God, unto whom all hearts are open, all desires known, and from whom no secrets are hid; cleanse the thoughts of our hearts by the inspiration of thy Holy Spirit, that we may perfectly love thee, and worthily magnify thy holy Name. (The Collect for Purity, Book of Common Prayer, page 67)

We live in an era of such incredible human-centeredness that even holy God is discussed and pictured by people with the most casual abandon in an abortive effort to reduce God to size, to total rational comprehensibility or to a thing or jargon, a gimmick, an illusory everyday convenience. Edmund Fuller caught something of this situation when he discussed Hipsterism in his book *Man in Modern Fiction:*

> Eternity comes cheaply here. It is found on the eyelids of a jazz musician. It was Miss Jane Russell, the well-known gospel singer, who dazzled us with the revelation that "God is a livin' doll." Now Kerouac, the hipster-theologian, in his final effusion, the closing lines of *On the Road*, tells us that "God is Pooh Bear."

This is end-of-paved-road in man's long history of awe and worship.[1]

Mr. Fuller reminds us that we need to recover alertness to awe, to grandeur, to the sense of the holy. Propaganda that proclaims the perverted virtues of this-worldly values is focused hard on human beings. It aims always to appeal to human egoism. People are always in the center of the stage—a god may be hovering in the wings or making an unimportant entrance to say a small line, but such a god may never intrude upon humankind's major speeches, dramatic histrionics, or big scenes.

Vivid pictures of the boredom and then the horror into which humankind can sink as if into quicksand are drawn by Paul Elmen in his book *The Restoration of Meaning to Contemporary Life.* The restoration of meaning in human life takes place when the glory of God replaces the boredom and the horror. Too, there is a true glory of humankind:

> It is the discovery of what a man truly is in the eyes of God. The glory of all created things is in their possibility of becoming what they really are, that is to say, what God meant them to be.[2]

Christian evangelism concerns God and God's love of humankind. *Evangelism* is an unpopular word today. Apparently it ought not to be in book titles, for books weighted down by the word *evangelism* on their jackets, one is told, will not sell. Not presently a smart word, obviously it is a misunderstood one; it is likely that it is wrongly synonymous in many minds with revivalism. Whatever the causes of its unpopularity, evangelism is badly in need of having a public relations job done for it. Does it need to be given a new, interesting package and put on a brand-new shelf so that it can be sold?

The basic ingredients of evangelism will not need to be changed at all, nor can they be changed. Christian evangelism is about God, who does not change. Evangelism that is Christian interestingly seems to fulfill the requirements of a basic rule of journalism demanding that five questions be answered in the lead paragraph of a good news story: who, what, when, where, how?

Christian evangelism answers these five basic questions about God's overwhelmingly great love for us, which caused God to send Jesus Christ into human life, to die for our sins upon the Cross and to be raised from the dead so that sin and death might be everlastingly vanquished, and then to send the Holy Comforter to be with us forever.

We do not altogether welcome this good news. The whole meaning of sin is self-love standing over against love of God. This good news of salvation breaks open human life, restores God's absolute centrality in clear focus, and calls for our response to God in love, trust, and thanksgiving. We are constantly tempted to focus on humankind instead of God, yet ironically it is only by focusing on God that human beings can bring themselves into clear, sharp focus. Evangelism often fails, indeed, for the very reason that the divine sovereignty of holy God in our lives is feared by people, who agitatedly cry that it represents intrusion. Obsessed by pride, we want to work out our destinies alone; but our destinies can be realized only in our relationship to God, our Creator and Redeemer.

The good news of God cannot be merchandised like a cereal, automobile, or movie, because the good news of God does not pander to human vanity and self-interest. It demands the response of the total person. It requires people's discovery of what they truly are in the eyes of God; this calls them to responsibility and destiny, away from childish things, their own will and way of doing things, even perhaps away from what they honestly may feel are their truest desires.

Religious huckstering places humankind in the center, in focus, with a manipulable, miraculous, technologically oriented God standing always ready to serve people in every way, from healing head colds to placing new cars in the garage, from winning track meets and beauty contests to establishing national supremacy for their own country in the world.

Evangelism—properly understood, so that the word is not just a caricature of evangelism—places God in the center, in focus. Because it does this, human beings are in focus, too—as they truly are in the eyes of God, as they stand in relation to holy God as children. Evangelism proclaims the good news that we are in the hand of the living God who cares enough (so completely) for us to redeem us whom God also created.

Christopher Fry, in his play A *Sleep of Prisoners*, sounds a note for a revivified evangelism in a few celebrated lines that take full cognizance of humankind's condition but, looking beyond human beings to God, are caught up in a tremendous surge of joy and hope:

The human heart can go to the lengths of God.
Dark and cold we may be, but this
Is no winter now. The frozen misery
Of centuries breaks, cracks, begins to move;
The thunder is the thunder of the floes,
The thaw, the flood, the upstart Spring.
Thank God our time is now when wrong

Comes up to face us everywhere,
Never to leave us till we take
The longest stride of soul men ever took.
Affairs are now soul size.
The enterprise
Is exploration into God.
What are you making for? It takes
So many thousand years to wake,
But will you wake for pity's sake?[3]

What is evangelism? A special commission appointed by
the General Board of the National Council of the Churches
of Christ in the U.S.A. defines it this way: "Evangelism is
making the Gospel known to those who do not know it, in
hope that they may be turned to God in faith, and making it
more effectively known to those who already live within the
Church, that their faith may grow in clarity and strength."

The Collect for Purity recognizes our own continual
need of evangelism and conversion. How are the thoughts
of our hearts purified? By intellectual activity? Good works?
Participation in more Church organizations? No; they are
purified by the inspiration of the Holy Spirit. The Holy
Spirit may work through intellectual activity or good works
or participation in more Church organizations, but God—
not we—will decide through what persons or activities God
wishes to operate. The agents on earth of God's will and
power in reaching us may be absolutely contrary to our
ideas of what agents God *should* use. (God even uses us,
when we haven't any idea that we are being used, as agents
of divine will and power in reaching others.)

The Holy Spirit is always the Evangelist, the Communi-
cator of the Holy Gospel. Enabled and guided by the
Spirit's inspiration, we become evangelists and communica-
tors of the Gospel. The Holy Spirit—the third Person of the

Trinity—is with us in every area of our lives, operating in and through persons and institutions, guiding, cleansing, strengthening, provoking mercy, and enabling love. Our communication of the Gospel is always commensurate with our own evangelization by the Gospel. Our showing forth of Christ in our lives is always commensurate with his conversion of us by the inspiration of the Holy Spirit.

Evangelism is more than we have too often defined it in practice. Quite honestly, it is *other* than we have too often defined it in practice.

Why do we ask God to cleanse the thoughts of our hearts by the inspiration of the Holy Spirit? So that we may perfectly love God and worthily magnify God's holy Name.

Perfect love of God transcends our imaginations, our profoundest desires, and our deepest communion with the Divine in worship. We do not reveal, in our individual and corporate lives, perfect love of God. Our Church life, by the mere fact of its being splintered and divided, denies our perfect love of God—for it is the fervent wish of Christ that the Church, his Body, be one ("The glory which thou hast given me I have given to them, that they may be one even as we are one, I in them and thou in me, that they may become perfectly one, so that the world may know that thou hast sent me and hast loved them even as thou hast loved me."— St. John 17:22–23). Too, our Church life, by its deviations from the divine will, by its lovelessness expressed both within the body and toward the world, by its too obvious desire to partake of the world's riches and prestige rather than the Way of the Cross of its Master, denies our perfect love of God. As a matter of fact, our love of God is a most imperfect thing. It is twisted into self-love. It expediently whines for mercy (being absorbed in self-pity) when it is merely waiting, once the divine blessing of forgiveness has been granted, to use God again in a flagrant denial of love.

God understands this perfectly. He sent the prophets, then his own Son into the world, to us, and we must confess that we know how we treated them all.

The important thing is that we confess our involvement in the human sin of turning away from God and God's holy will, instead of offering excuses for ourselves (*"I* didn't rebuff any of the prophets"; *"I* didn't crucify Christ"; *"I* am not responsible for any racial hatred"; *"I* can honestly say that I have never hurt anybody"). After confessing our involvement in the human sin of turning away from God, and "with hearty repentance and true faith" turning unto God, the important thing is that we earnestly pray that God will increase in us the divine grace of love. We cannot give up simply because, again and again, our love of God is found to be imperfect; we must press on as persons who run a race, confidently hoping and seeking that we may perfectly love God.

Our evangelism will reflect, always, the degree of our confidently hoping and seeking that we may perfectly love God. When we no longer hope and seek after this, our evangelism loses its fervor, warmth, and dynamic. It becomes dry and mechanical.

What else do we ask the Holy Spirit to accomplish in us, when the thoughts of our hearts are cleansed? First, we ask that we might be enabled perfectly to love God. In addition, we ask that we may "worthily magnify" God's holy Name.

When we pray this we are asking that our lives may somehow, by God's grace, show forth the divine glory; that our actions may reflect God's love within us; that our lives may honor rather than dishonor God; that our lives may, in fact, by the emptying of our natural self-centeredness and the sacrifice of our humanly most obvious selfish interests, magnify God's holy Name by revealing the extent of the divine power to transform our lives from self-propelled mechanisms into harmonious unities of body, mind, and soul freely offered to God for the work of the Realm.

How often the "good" churchly people are seen standing over against the "bad" unchurched people, whom the "good" people are going to evangelize! This picture of the morally self-righteous, not beclouded by any sense of sin at all, going out to do battle for Christ by bringing into the fold the "bad" people, has been enough to keep large numbers from seeking or accepting fellowship in the Church. The pronouncement "we sinners," instead of the pronouncement "you sinners," not only works wonders in catching a hearer's attention; it also works wonders in softening the hardness of our own hearts.

We churched folk have not ceased to be sinners because we are members of the Church. We have, as members of the Church, begun to understand the meaning of sin (separation from God) and to realize the labyrinths of sin within ourselves. We have also, as members of the Church, been introduced to the forgiveness of sin. We comprise the perfect democracy of sinners; we know this and accept ourselves as sinners—and, too, as forgiven sinners. We ought never to be cast down or defeated by sin or Satan, because we are always being forgiven by God when we come to God with repentance and faith and express our desire to be forgiven and to amend our lives.

Humankind used to think there was hope in mankind. The "good life"—a cocoon-like existence, selfish, passive, placid—was a definite ideal, partially realized. Then came the technological revolution, two World Wars, the Bomb; the world was changed, and humankind living in the world was changed, too. People realize that they are not (as on a curve) making slow but real progress in the world. They are aware of the contradiction that lies beneath the false happy-face symbol of the "good life."

People need other people to help them look away from themselves, toward God. Those who have turned away from the Church because they rejected an awful caricature of the Church that had been shown to them (perhaps by a Church or Church member) need others to be evangelists to them. Church members cannot be these needed evangelists except by the power of God the Holy Spirit indwelling them and causing them to press forward here and to pause there, cleansing their thoughts so that they may more perfectly show forth the love of God to those outside the Church needing evangelists, needing to be shown how to love God and to magnify God's holy Name.

Is not this how evangelism works? On an intensely personal level, relating *this* person to *that* person, and doing this in the dynamic power of the *Holy Spirit* who alone can accomplish the "relating"?

We have become such literalists! We have to be *shown,* in black and white, and everything must be obvious, on the surface! Yet God works mysteriously in divine ways that are other than human ways. God's paths elude our human radar devices. I found an interesting analogy to this in photography. Richard Avedon, the excellent fashion photographer, was the subject of a Profile by Winthrop Sargeant in the *New Yorker* titled "A Woman Entering a Taxi in the Rain." Mr. Avedon told Mr. Sargeant:

> I began trying to create an out-of-focus world—a heightened reality better than real, that suggests, rather than tells you. Maybe the fact I'm myopic had something to do with it. When I take off my glasses, especially on rainy nights, I get a far more beautiful view

of the world than twenty-twenty people get. I wanted to reproduce this more poetic image that I was privately enjoying.[4]

Mr. Avedon experimented with a technical device in which the blur is used deliberately as a means of poetic evocation.

When I first read about this I said to myself that Mr. Avedon was only fooling himself, really, and that he was, in effect, "looking at the world through rose-colored glasses." Then I realized that Mr. Avedon has instead undoubtedly reached a deeper-than-surface level of reality. He has, in his own area of activity, partially corrected a fault common to most of us.

We have all become largely indifferent to reality. We have assumed that reality is what appears to be or what the eye (or mind) detects. Actually, however, when we stop to think about it, we discover that reality is often quite the opposite of what appears to be, or what can be detected by the eye or the mind. People cover up their real feelings; beauty is hidden; the real motive escapes notice; the real wish is buried. A heightened reality may not only grasp our attention but stimulate and challenge us. Far more important, a heightened reality may enable us to discern the layer upon layer of reality underlying what merely appears on the surface to be reality.

In evangelism, and in our work as evangelists of Christ and his Gospel, one of the great dangers confronting us is our penchant for being literalists, for believing that anything *real* (in this case, *real* evangelism or *real* conversion) must be obvious and on the surface. Actually, *real* evangelism and *real* conversion (known, of course, only to God if they are *real*) will always be largely hidden, largely mysterious, elusive of our literalist, emphatic labels. In our evangelism we may be blessed to plant seeds of conversion or to nurture the growth of such seeds that have already been planted. Seldom will we plant, nurture, and reap the harvest of conversion. Seldom can we proudly point to an exhibit of our evangelistic success, saying, "There, *I* am responsible for that conversion." The convert may "fall" shortly thereafter, to our distinct embarrassment and his or hers; the convert's momentary failure would not be indicative of our failure (any more than the convert's not "falling" would be indicative of our success). We simply do not measure evangelism in such ways. One cannot be statistical about evangelism. It is the work of the Holy Spirit—hidden, working now through *this* human agent, now through *that* human agent, mysterious always to us who do not see things as God sees things. Ironically, an out-of-focus world (like the one photographer Richard Avedon has experimented with) may be more *in focus*, in terms of essential underlying reality, than an apparently in-focus world! So with our work as evangelists. What appears to be may not be at all, and what does not appear on the surface may be the key to understanding. What of Christ's death on the Cross? Did he appear to be the Lord of heaven and earth, or a dying wreckage of a man? Did his Cross appear to be the means of salvation for all people, or a sordid and common instrument of torture and execution for slaves? "Now faith is the assurance of things hoped for, the conviction of things not seen" (Hebrews 11:1). We do not, as Christians, perceive with our eyes that which is reality; we perceive reality only by faith.

For this reason, we acknowledge and confess before God our inability to serve God at all by means of our own resources or abilities. We ask God to cleanse the thoughts of our hearts by the inspiration of the Holy Spirit, that we may perfectly love God and worthily magnify God's holy Name— as God's evangelists in the world where God has placed us.

II. The Revolution in Evangelism

Thou shalt love the Lord thy God with all thy heart, and with all thy soul, and with all thy mind. . . . Thou shalt love thy neighbor as thyself. (From the Summary of the Law, 1928 Book of Common Prayer, page 69)

Evangelism is our *duty*. Love of God requires expression of that love in proclaiming its existence to, and sharing it with, others. Genuine love of God will, of itself, manifest itself in communication. The two great commandments are indissolubly linked, for the natural expression of love of God *is* love of one's neighbor.

Who is my neighbor? Anyone. Anyone in need, or close to me, or who enters—however briefly—into my life or line of vision. The definition is limitless. One of the hardest aspects of urban life is that one lives in such close proximity to so many persons who exist in indifference, isolation, and the most acute kind of loneliness, that of feeling essentially and terribly alone while being actually in a crowd. One can identify oneself easily with *Doctor Zhivago* when, toward the conclusion of the Pasternak novel, the tired old man is riding a Moscow streetcar. He suffers a heart attack. He meets no response of compassion or help at all, but only hardness, ridicule, and bitterness. Zhivago is, at this moment, a member of the lonely crowd. Urbanized culture, in Moscow or New York, Johannesburg or Paris, has had to learn how not to care. It has learned it well.

The Summary of the Law states its absolute demand in lean language: ". . . with all thy heart, and with all thy soul, and with all thy mind." It is good we have first prayed to God to cleanse the thoughts of our hearts by the inspiration of the Holy Spirit. We prayed that God might enable us to love God and worthily magnify God's holy Name. How fortunate for us that we could say this prayer before we found ourselves confronted by the Summary of the Law, with its clear demands that one cannot squirm out of. Of course, we know now that the only way we may hope to love God as God deserves—or, obey God's Law as God commands—is by God's own Spirit ruling our hearts, guiding our wills, enabling us to love and obey God.

The Summary of the Law makes it unmistakably clear that evangelism is not a hobby or something we *may* do if we like, or even a hard "good work" we may choose to do if we want to be extraordinarily fine Christians. *Evangelism is the duty of every Christian.* All Christians are called to be evangelists of the Savior Jesus. Nominal Christians by choice may remain unbothered by the Law of God; they are Christians in name only. Sadly, they may, just by indifferently carrying the name "Christian," do untold harm to the cause of Christian evangelism, for many people will hear the "preaching" of such Christians' lives and discover that it does not jibe with the seriousness of the preaching of the Gospel. Merely nominal Christians may consider evangelism to be a bother and a bore, and feel that it is outside the pale of their concern and interest. Practicing Christians accept evangelism not only as a duty but as a privilege. Yes, they may become both bothered *and* bored as they sometimes painfully pursue the vocation of evangelist, but such passing feelings will not affect their commitment and discipleship. Anyhow, they have learned to offer such feelings—along with those of joy and stimulation—to Christ, and to get on with the business at hand.

Evangelism requires us to offer God our bodies and souls *and minds.* A number of people persist in withholding their minds from God's service. "Can't I just move by blind faith without using my mind? Must I relate the faith to the world around me? This is too much work!" This reaction unfortunately fits a large number of nominal Christians. In *The Faith of the Church,* James A. Pike and W. Norman Pittenger succinctly spoke to this problem in the historical setting of the early Church:

> But because the Christians, like all other human beings, lived in the world of men and affairs, and above all because of their pagan environment, they were obliged to think about their faith. They were obliged to relate it to the rest of their experience. Theological development was bound to take place and did in fact take place immediately.[1]

Theology is not an esoteric word, or one held captive by an elite. It is simply our study of the existence and nature of God. It is, in effect, what we understand and know about God. Evangelism requires the development of theology in every age and culture. For example, in our own age and culture we must develop theology that relates God's sovereignty and providence, the redemptive sacrifice of Jesus Christ, and the sustaining power of God the Holy Spirit to sharply accentuated urbanization, the space age, mass communications, and nuclear warfare.

Of course, having offered God our minds does not automatically mean that we have offered God our bodies and souls. It is entirely possible to intellectualize about the Christian life and fail to live it. The Summary of the Law proclaims the *total demand* of God upon the *total life* of human beings: body, soul, and mind.

Our duty is to love. One cannot really love out of a sense of duty, however, but only in love itself. Love is a gift of God that enables us to pass on the same love to other persons; we have only to be open channels to receive God's love and, instead of bottling it up, to let it flow through us to other men, women, and children. In fact, we cannot bottle up God's love, even if we should like to. It cannot be imprisoned or manipulated. It uses us for the work of evangelism, but we cannot use it for selfish reasons.

How do we love? Another way of asking the same question is, *how* do we evangelize?

There has been a revolution in our time, within Church life, having to do with evangelism. Evangelism is, in fact, making the Gospel known to those who do not know it. Methods of accomplishing this have been radically altered and are in the process of even more radical revision. The reason is evident. In Europe, an evident post-Christian society has manifested itself. And in the United States, a seeming religious revival coupled with a good deal of cultural religiosity has obscured a hard core of intelligent, determined opposition to the Christian faith here. It was Truman B. Douglass who pointed out that Christianity has failed to penetrate three major areas in our time: Islam, Hinduism, and city life.

I have seen the hard "post-Christian" signs evident in the inner city of a major American city where I have been rector of a parish in a disintegrating neighborhood of rapid social change.

I recall, too, a dramatic, overwhelming awareness of the

sheer size of apartment buildings erected in New York City in a slum-clearance area. Each of these buildings houses more people than live in many small Mid-western towns—towns having three or four churches each. In these apartment buildings in New York, there is neither a church nor a chaplain. There is no Christian strategy of penetration, and the buildings seem to be hard shells almost protecting the occupants from the intrusion of the Gospel. How can we break through such structures in order to reach the individual men, women, and children inside them? How can we break through the equally hard-shell structures of industry and professions, themselves encased within the super-structure of the metropolis?

The Church is coming up with experiments and new strategies to meet the needs posed by these questions. I have studied first-hand some of these. In England, I spent some time visiting the Church of England's Industrial Mission at Sheffield under Canon E. R. Wickham, and the parish of St. Wilfrid's, Halton, Leeds, where the House-Church movement has been developed.[2]

In the summer of 1957, I spent several months living and working in the French Community of Taizé. This ecumenically oriented community regards the world as its "monastery" and it sends *frères* out to work in industry and to relate the Gospel to widely varying problems of modern life. Evangelism, for the *frères* of Taizé, is linked with a strong sense of the presence of Christ in members of his mystical Body who, entering into the world and engaging in different kinds of work and sharing solidarity with others in such work, represent *Jesus Christ* in the milieu in which they live. I remember the question raised by one *frère* concerning which kind of activity is "highly evangelistic" and which type of activity is "less evangelistic"; for example, is a *frère* who conducts a retreat being a better evangelist than a *frère* who is working as a ceramist, or as a member of the village civil-community council, or on the farm at Taizé, or as a physician?

One man whose presence in a strategic area for nearly forty years has represented, for Christians and non-Christians alike, the presence of Christ in their situation is an Anglican priest, the Rev. St. John B. Groser. His area has been the East End of London, in the former slum section of Stepney. He has long pioneered in the work of bridging the gap between the working-class world and the Church. In 1926, when the famous General Strike broke out in England, Fr. Groser participated as a priest in the citizens' march on Trafalgar Square. During the same strike he was trying to keep police from charging a crowd of men, women, and children in Stepney when his hand was broken by a club. When workers in one mass unemployment march on London saw Fr. Groser in his clerical suit, several of them started singing derisively, "You'll get pie in the sky when you die." The institutional Church was not identified with the working class and these workers assumed that Fr. Groser was there either to mutter platitudes or simply to observe them. But a worker from East London cried: "Stop it! He's one of us!"

Father Groser lived in Stepney through the bitter days of violence, the wartime Blitz with its heavy bombings of East London, and the postwar years. Now he is Master of the Royal Foundation of St. Katharine. It was my privilege to spend a month with Fr. Groser and his associates at the Foundation a couple of years ago. Father Groser's work to-day is exploring the meaning of work itself, trying to define responsibility and personal relationships in work. Fr. Groser recalls one incident from the violent prewar days in Stepney when a non-Christian said to him, "If only you didn't be-lieve in God, what a good labor leader you'd make. You

sense people's needs." Father Groser replied, "That's because I believe in God." Father Groser was a forerunner of
the Wickhams and Southcotts of today who, in their own
ways, are responding in the same tradition to contemporary
problems with radically contemporary, relevant methods.

Throughout the world one finds people and movements
rising up to meet the challenge of effective evangelism for
our own time. The Zoë Movement has come out of the rigid
mold of the Church in Greece, representing a decided fer-
ment and an outbreak of new ideas about the relation of
faith and culture. When I talked with several leaders of the
Zoë Movement in Athens, they assured me that Zoë
stresses, above everything else, the Church's sacramental
life. The movement is strikingly lay-inspired. It comprises an
assorted mixture of elements, it has a puritan strand, it
strives to remain solidly within the Church, yet it attracts
large numbers of people who are both loyal to their faith
and dissatisfied with some present conditions in the
Church. Zoë represents an attempt to speak to the vast
nominally Christian public without neglecting the Church's
language of liturgy and sacrament.

The Greek Orthodox Church is strongly represented
within the Ecumenical Movement. When His Holiness the
Ecumenical Patriarch of Constantinople received me for
conversation and luncheon at Istanbul, he reflected a concern for the unity of the world's Christians as intense as I
have noticed in any ecumenical leader. Christians of all
Churches are becoming aware of the necessity for a common Christian strategy and a united Christian voice in the
face of post-Christianity and fragmented witness in missionary endeavor. I spent some months at the Ecumenical
Institute of the World Council of Churches, the Château de
Bossey, in Switzerland. Here, young Christians from all
parts of the world and differing Church traditions lived and

studied together and met, head on, the "ecumenical problem." I noted down my conclusions about this problem in *Crisis in Communication:*

> The Ecumenical Movement is clearly not a watering-down process, a compromise in terms of sacrificing essential elements of faith, an idealistic attempt to arrive at a unity at any cost, or a pressurized steam-rolling process. It is realized that the unity of the Church will not be achieved in terms of wishful thinking or by being moved emotionally. Nor will it be achieved by a few individuals who attempt to jump individually over fences, leaving their brethren behind. The individual's share in the corporate sin of division must be borne, not lightly set aside in a sentimental way. "Bless God for the hard lessons learned at Bossey, as well as for the more readily discernible riches." Thus Suzanne de Dietrich spoke in a retreat closing the 1954–55 graduate school at Bossey.[3]

The Ecumenical Movement is basically a human response to divine love. It is evangelistic in essence, growing out of a realization that the evangelism of the Church is disastrously stymied by such disparate Christian voices speaking to world culture in the name of Christ. It is interesting to note an ecumenical compulsion within the Roman Catholic Church, which is not a member of the World Council of Churches (in which Anglicanism has played a dominant role from its inception). Father George H. Tavard, a prominent spokesman of Roman Catholic ecumenism, speaks of the vocation of the ecumenist of his Church as being "to make the Church and the separated communions mutually understandable." Father M. J. Congar, the French Dominican, states: "It is becoming no longer a question of confessional differences within Christendom itself, but of a radical choice between the Kingdom of God and the reign of Antichrist." Roman Catholic ecumenism envisions reunion in terms of the "return" of non-Romans to the Roman Church. It was a privilege I shall always recall with profound gratitude to be invited to spend several weeks with the Dominicans in Paris at Istina, the celebrated Roman Catholic study center. At Istina, a continuous study is made of ecumenical activities throughout the world and a major contribution is offered in ecumenical scholarship. A publication, *Istina,* is issued by Father Dumont and his associates.

Evangelism requires finding and establishing points of contact with the unchurched. It must result in a breakthrough—through alien cultures and the vacuum of outmoded Christian words and symbols in post-Christianity—to people with whom the Church has no facile, obvious, or ready-at-hand point of contact. The Church is finding one area of breakthrough in art forms. The explicitly "religious" drama (on television or the stage or movie screen) does not often result in a breakthrough, but drama that has an implicit Christian significance or lends itself to a striking Christian interpretation may provide an immensely valuable point of contact with many people completely alienated from the life of the Church.[4]

I have noticed considerable work in this field being done in the Church's college work recently. For example, when I was convocation speaker at Religious Emphasis Week at Louisiana State University in the spring of 1959, one of the chaplains there played a leading role in a student presentation of the play *Sign of Jonah.* The preceding year, during Religious Emphasis Week, the student presentation was Jean-Paul Sartre's one-act picture of hell, *No Exit.*

In West Berlin, I saw a presentation of *Die Vaganten,* a dramatic group that is organized under Christian principles. I attended its presentation of a nihilist drama by the late Wolfgang Borchert entitled *Draussen vor der Tür (Outside the Door)*. Its director, Horst Behrendt, explained how *Die Vaganten* makes use of both explicit and implicit religious drama. This particular ten-year-old play depicts the return to Germany, in 1945, of a soldier who finds everything in life closed against him. Even suicide offers no real alternative, and life is meaningless, distorted, and altogether mad. The Christian dramatic group presented the play because, as the program stated, it is drama that no theater wants to produce and no public wishes to see, yet it is drama that Germany needs to see, if it is to take seriously the task of comprehending itself. *Die Vaganten's* effort is a radical example of finding a point of contact for the Gospel.

One could offer many, many more examples of evangelistic adaptation to the needs and conditions of our age and culture. In foreign missionary work itself, a great effort is being made to emphasize the sending of native Christian missionaries, for example, rather than missionaries who, by the color of their skin or their speech or their education, bear witness to another culture. In the United States, there are enough scattered and significant experiments in evangelism to fill a book.

The duty of being evangelists is increasingly being emphasized within the Church in new and compelling ways.

III. The Lordship of Christ over the Totality of Life

Holy, Holy, Holy, Lord God of hosts, Heaven and earth are full of thy glory: Glory be to thee, O Lord Most High. Amen. (The Sanctus, 1928 Book of Common Prayer, page 77)

We are to claim for God what is God's. The totality of human life belongs to God. We are called upon to preach Christ's Gospel of Salvation to all humankind and to all conditions of humankind.

In the *Sanctus* we acknowledge the holiness, the "otherness," the purity, and the exaltedness of God. In a mighty paean of praise, we cry that all of life in heaven and earth is full of God's glory. Then we offer all of this, God's glory, back to God.

One of the most disastrous mistakes that is made in much Christian witness and evangelism is accepting the brokenness of the world and human life into separate, airtight compartments, unrelated to God and to one another. "Religion" is made one "department" of life (as it is made one "department" of the news in the newsmagazines). Therefore, "Books" becomes a department, and "Business" and "Foreign Affairs" and "Art" and "Science." It is very easy, once such compartmentalization begins, just to be led along mentally until one fails to see the relationship of "Religion" to "Science," for example, or of "Religion" to "Business." It is obvious in American life that very, very few people do see the relationship of the Christian faith (which they may profess) to their business ethics, for example, or to the world of science that intrigues them and challenges their imaginations.

I had great difficulty seeing the relationship of the Christian faith to the other component parts of God's world when I first entered seminary to begin my studies for the Episcopal priesthood. I was leaving the world of communications and the field of entertainment. I remember that a priest said to me: "Now one door is closing for you. Another door is opening. *You are leaving one world and going into another world.*"

Nearly everyone I knew seemed to feel that way about it. The two "worlds" would not collide, it was felt; they were seen to be in vastly different orbits, far away from each other.

I had been a successful person in the world of movies, television, and motion pictures in New York and Hollywood. I was leaving that world to enter an Episcopal seminary. Was I going into another world? At a very large and sentimental "going-away" luncheon given for me in Hollywood I realized, but could not understand precisely why, a kind of door was somehow closing in my life. The known seemed to be clustered in an isolated island in my past, and in my present, which was so rapidly becoming my past. The unknown seemed, at that moment, to be the chief distinguishing mark of my life.

Hedda Hopper wrote in her syndicated column that the Picture of the Week occurred at the luncheon when everybody in Ciro's, including two bartenders, stood for the com-

mon recitation of the Lord's Prayer. There was a garish, vul-
gar note in the luncheon party, in its very sentimentality, its
dramatization, indeed, its simplification of some extremely
complex factors. Yet one was struck surprisingly by a pro-
foundly underlying strength of purpose in the mere fact of
this meeting; people were saying things and giving rein to
feelings they ordinarily would securely hide from their co-
hort sophisticates; there was a refreshing simplicity, and a
brightness and expectancy, in some ordinarily tired, jaded
faces. For Hollywood, a most unusual thing happened: top
stars were seated alongside bit players, top producers alongside low-rung studio employees. There was, momentarily, a
fusion of interests and intentions, a unity of spirit in the
crowd that assembled to see a young coworker off to (of all
unlikely places) a theological seminary.

During the years that have passed since the luncheon, I
have increasingly felt that there was an unfortunate aspect
of the whole event. I was seen as going away, in a dreadful
severing of human ties. A number of persons wept, and this
was due to sentimental and "religious" connotations, but
also to the unconscious feeling that they were somehow at-
tending my funeral; after this, I would be dead to them, they
felt. There was a finality in this "goodbye."

Three days after the luncheon, I drove my car from Los
Angeles to Berkeley, to enter the Church Divinity School of
the Pacific for three years. The hundreds of friends and ac-
quaintances of mine in communications in New York and
Hollywood; the hundreds of experiences I had of the
"world" of advertising, public relations, films, television:
were these now to be cut surgically from my life? How deep
would the scalpel have to cut? Was this God's will?

There had been questions from the moment my intention to leave the communications world for seminary was
announced in the press. Why was I making so drastic a

change in my life? Some persons felt that they understood my new sense of vocation, blessed by the Church, which was leading me into radical changes in my life. My telephone rang incessantly: "I had wanted to be a priest but. . ."; "I had wanted to study to be a rabbi but. . ."; "I felt a call to Christian service, many years ago, but. . . ." Façades were dropped and I felt I knew, for the first time, some persons with whom I had worked for years.

Others were sure that I was simply terribly confused, tired, sick, or about to be crushed by the impact of an experience I could not possibly understand. A reporter from the *San Francisco Chronicle*, I remember, waited to interview me the same day I reached the seminary. He, too, was waiting to ask, "Why?" It was in this atmosphere that I entered upon my seminary days.

Many persons I had known felt that I would henceforth live a "cloistered life" (in my interests, duties, tastes, attitudes) absolutely unrelated to the flow of life in our time. They felt that I would speak another language that would render communication between us impossible. Some feared that I would judge them self-righteously; others simply expected to be judged (and rightly, they said). Some sincerely believed that henceforth I should speak an altogether different language than I had spoken or they spoke. The implication, therefore, was that I could not continue to "speak their language." So began the agonizing process of relating *this* to *that*, and everything to the sovereignty of Christ.

I had to learn how to relate my work in communications with my work as a theological student, but how was I to go about it? As long as I looked upon life as being composed of airtight compartments or unrelated "worlds," I could not comprehend or work out any realistic Christian theology.

After a year, I came to realize—with the sudden and wonderful shock of a momentous discovery that one makes in his or her own experience, unoriginal though the discovery may be for others—that all of life is a part of one world, and it is all in the hand of the living God. The sovereignty of Jesus Christ is exercised over the totality of human life and experience. Nothing, absolutely nothing, is unrelated either to Christ or to the other component parts that go to make up this one world.

It was suddenly apparent to me that I had not left one "world" at all in order to enter another "world." I had simply ceased to exercise one function in the world in order to exercise another function in the same world. (Later, I would be able to understand that *either* function, that of television producer or priest, may be an active ministry in the Church. I would later come to realize, moreover, that a television producer's Christian ministry would not in any way be limited to the making of "religious" programs. It would, instead, depend on the producer's *being a Christian.*) Quite fundamentally, I had been enabled to perceive the fact of one world because I had, first, been enabled to perceive the reign of Jesus Christ over all of human life and concern. There are not many "worlds." There are many parts of one world.

I recall the letter a public accountant in the Midwest wrote to me after reading a newspaper story about my entering seminary. He asked the question so many persons were asking: "Why?" He went further: "Shouldn't you have remained on the firing line? Why did you run away from the combat? Couldn't you, as a Christian, have done more good as a layman active in the communications field?"

At the time, I could not answer him. I felt that I had been called to be a priest in the Church, and that was that: how else could I explain myself to this letter writer? Now, I have come to see, in Europe and America, the concept of the Christian frontier: the no man's land between Church and world where Christian laypersons are called to do daily labor for Christ. I see now that the Christian frontier is the vocation of practicing Christian laypersons, to show forth their faith *where they are in the world.* Yet I still—and more strongly—believe that my own particular calling was to function, in my Christian ministry, as a priest in the Church.

It seems to me that it is of the utmost importance to realize that all Christians, in whatever ministry they may be exercising, are ministering in God's name and power and love to any part of the totality of human life and experience which comes their way. A grave error would be compounded if the layperson's ministry were seen to be "in the world" with the clergy's ministry being solely "in the Church." Always, due partially to the cultural and professional upper-middle-class status frequently accorded the clergy in our society and time, and the narrow niche given them in that august spectrum, there is a tendency for the clergy to be snowed under by intramural churchly matters that keep them from their more important duty to preach the Gospel not only within the Church but out in the world.

The Gospel does not ever exist in a vacuum; it exists in the world. It is to be preached in, and to, the world. The preacher is scrupulously to avoid being of the world (under the world's standards and values, in thralldom to the world's rewards) while emphatically at all times being *in* the world (which has been created by God, redeemed by Jesus Christ, indwelt by the Holy Spirit).

This is always a difficult and cagey tension—being *in,* but not *of,* the world. I have experienced this tension myself under most difficult circumstances. A further bit of personal biography may serve to illustrate the point of this Christian tension that is common, in one form or another, to all who are trying to live the Christian life in the world.

In my own case, after having been unable to relate my previous work in life with what had become my present work in life, suddenly there came the moment when I could see relatedness between the two in Christ. Consequently, I continued to develop my interest in communications, as a seminary student, but quite sharply with a new Christian orientation. I took very seriously the work of appearing on "religious" television programs, writing articles about the relation of Christian theology and communications, and acting in an advisory capacity to a producer of motion pictures and filmstrips that were based on religious personalities and themes. Frequently, in those days, I was interviewed by motion picture and television reporters about my new ideas. All this created a tension, I realized to my dismay and embarrassment. Many people could not understand: was I going to be a priest or a communications "expert," a television producer, a public relations specialist? "One must be one or the other." So, I was right back in my old dilemma of two different "worlds," only now I had at least worked out a basic theology proclaiming the sovereignty of Christ over the unity of God's creation, and I was enabled to live under the criticism and misunderstanding that confronted me.

While studying in England and on the Continent, after my graduation from seminary in California, new intellectual concepts entered with considerable dynamic force into my experience. I realized, with new awareness, that Christians in communications need not be concerned solely with "religious" television, radio, film, and press media, but may choose other tasks in Christian strategy. They may seek to penetrate the "principalities and powers" that institutionally provide a context for communications work; they may simply try to present a Christian witness—to preach the Gospel in life terms and nonverbal terms—*where they are,* working in a movie studio or a television production office, an advertising agency or a newspaper or magazine office. Or, they may concentrate their interest in preparing and producing communications material that contains an *implicit* (but not an explicit) Christian proclamation.

I have tried to write about communications, as a Christian. This work developed out of my conviction that the men and women functioning in the complex media of mass communication should come to understand better the men and women of the Church, and the faith of the Church to which they assent and for which they are evangelists. I felt it was equally important for the Christians of our day to know better the men and women who are operating the great new technological instruments of communications, and the ideas underlying their work. Communication surely remains the task of both groups. Both groups are one in Christ.

The initial draft of my first book, *Crisis in Communication,* was written in Switzerland. It was completed for publication at Union Theological Seminary in New York City where, as a tutor assistant, I wrote my second book, *Christ and Celebrity Gods.* During these years I wrote numerous magazine articles relating the Christian faith and our culture.

I had retreated from actual personal involvement in communications to a vantage point from which I wrote and spoke as a critic. I was critical of some Christians in communications work who were busily using such media as television, radio, films, and the press, yet, in my opinion, were really misusing these media because they neglected to lay any theological groundwork for their energetic efforts. They seemed not to comprehend the dangerous pitfalls in "exploitation" masquerading as "evangelism." At the same time, I was critical of other influential Christian leaders who refused to use these mass media. They were singularly failing, in my opinion, to relate the holiness of God to mass media, which are God's instruments in the modern technological world. I considered the latter group to be as theologically unsound as the former seemed to be theologically unaware.

Professor Hendrik Kraemer of Bossey, Canon Theodore O. Wedel of the College of Preachers in Washington, D.C., Professor John Bachman of Union Theological Seminary in New York City, Dean Sherman E. Johnson of the Church Divinity School of the Pacific in Berkeley, California, Professors Reinhold Niebuhr and John C. Bennett of New York—these, and others, shaped my thinking about the theology of communications, challenging me and forcing me to discard obsolete ideas and to incorporate new ones into my work. As a result, I was gradually enabled to balance my work as critic of mass communications with a new role as participant in mass communications. I narrated a coast-to-coast radio program, *Pilgrimage,* for the National Council of Churches and made numerous radio and television guest appearances on different programs. There had been a time in my theological development when I wrongly withdrew from participation in the field of communications. Now, I was patiently led, in Christian love, into relevant and hard participation.

One night in 1958 I came to be sitting in a New York television studio. Streams of light shone dramatically upon two men seated across the studio. The cameras recorded their every movement, caught every subtlety of expression and, seemingly, recorded every thought passing through their minds. In a few minutes I would take the place of one of the men and become the subject of a "depth interview" on the controversial *Night Beat* program. In my opinion, did participation in a television program like this one constitute valid evangelism?

I was waiting—seven years after entering seminary—to

discuss, in a few minutes, the Christian faith on a great medium of mass communication. I was now rooted in my work as a parish priest; I had been enabled by the Church to understand my ministry as partaking vocationally of the necessity to interpret contemporary culture in the light of the Christian faith; I had been sent by the Church, in fact, to be a Christian apologist in the speeding, tense, charged, expectant arena of modern life that lay exposed before my eyes in the form of the great television studio. I now clearly understood that it is the responsibility and vocation of the Church to be as concerned with baptizing culture as with baptizing babies.

Waiting to go before the television cameras, I knew that I had been called by God, acting through the Church, to this moment. I tried to offer God all about the moment that seemed good, all that seemed ambiguous, all that seemed evil. I waited as an evangelist, forgiven, endowed, sent by God to be God's example of servanthood in this place. A television man raised his hand to summon me to take my position. I stood up and started walking toward the cameras.

"Lord, be on my lips and in my understanding." Isn't this what we must always pray, as we undertake the hard-core evangelism of preaching both to Church and world the integral, solid relationship of the holiness and glory of God with all the things of this life and world that God has created to be used for God's glory?

IV. The "What" of the Gospel

Take, eat, this is my Body, which is given for you. . . .
Drink ye all of this; for this is my Blood of the New Testa-
ment, which is shed for you, and for many, for the remission
of sins. . . . (From the Prayer of Consecration, 1928
Book of Common Prayer, page 80)

It has been said that too much emphasis is placed in the
Church on the "how" of evangelism, the methods and techniques to be employed for communicating the Gospel.
More important than the "how," it is claimed, is the "what"
of the Gospel. What *is* the Gospel that we, as evangelists, are
communicating to others?

The Gospel is the good news that Jesus Christ has saved
us from sin and death. The Son of God has shared our hu-
manity, has lived human life (though without sin), has died
on the Cross for our sakes, has risen from the dead to overcome the power of death for the salvation of all, has as-
cended to the Father, and has sent us the Holy Comforter,
to be with us always.

The heart of the Christian Gospel is the sacrifice of
Christ for our salvation. In the Holy Eucharist—the means
of communion with Jesus that he instituted on the night in

which he was betrayed—Christ is with us in the sacrament of his Body and Blood. This sacrament is the means he has left us for our being united with him, whereby we may indwell him, and he us. Holy Baptism and the Holy Communion are the two sacraments that the Church instructs us are necessary for salvation; as such, they are the very cornerstones of evangelism. In Holy Baptism we are baptized into Christ's death and eternal life, and become members of his Body, the Church. In the Holy Communion Jesus comes to us in the wondrous act of communion that is sanctified by God's linking the divine and the human.

For the Church and the world, this is the sacrifice— "once offered . . . full, perfect, and sufficient . . . for the sins of the whole world." This sacrifice of Jesus Christ is the means of salvation for the whole world. Naturally, our evangelism will be anchored in the "what" of this sacrifice.

The Person and the work of Jesus Christ are what all our evangelism should really be about. Our techniques and our constantly new efforts to establish points of contact with unchurched persons are all directed toward communicating the meaning of the Person and the work of Jesus Christ in winning salvation for all on the Cross. In our evangelism we strive to make "relevant" the sacrifice of Jesus Christ by making clear its direct connection with people's everyday life, their work and leisure, ethical decisions and moral problems, politics and cultural interests.

It is the capping irony, in many ways, that the men and women for whose redemption Christ has died on the Cross need to be reminded of his very "relevance" to them and their lives! Yet such is the actual condition; we cannot gloss it over or rationalize it away by wishful thinking. Adding to our difficulty in establishing the "relevance" of Christ to every human life (and the life of every society, of every culture) is that Christ has been preached for so long to people who are deaf and indifferent to the preaching. "Oh, yes, I know all about that," a nominal Christian may say about the Church's proclamation of the Christmas or Easter event. Yet nominal Christians are merely seeing without perceiving, merely hearing without comprehending, merely knowing a set of facts without knowing their meaning for *them*. Again, we have to make a major breakthrough for the Gospel, this time cutting through mental blocks and psychological hazards instead of through institutions and walls of mighty housing developments.

How are we to do it?

Any preacher knows the extreme difficulty inherent in the familiar, often close to stereotype, Christmas or Easter sermon. The people who are never otherwise in church will be on hand, all decked out for the season's festivities and also perhaps desperately longing deep inside—well hidden by a façade of bravado or sophistication—for *the good news of God*. ("Speak to me this Christmas, I need it so badly. If there's any truth to this, let me have it today, this Easter. I'm just about beat. Is there freshness, something new, something real, an honest message of hope? O possibility of God, O possibility of Christ . . . God, Christ . . . help me . . . have mercy. . . .)

But so often, the breakthrough does not happen. Or, if it does, it is not recognized. Or, if it is recognized, it is rejected amid fear and guilt and longing, because it *is* so demanding: "Can't there be the good news of God without the Cross?"

British playwright John Osborne, in his first "angry" play, *Look Back in Anger,* reflects the final condition of the failure of all attempts at breakthrough to reach his central character, in these lines:

Nobody thinks, nobody cares. No beliefs, no convictions, and no enthusiasm. Just another Sunday evening.[1]

One realizes, when reading Tennessee Williams's play *Sweet Bird of Youth*, that there have been tragically abortive efforts to establish a breakthrough of the saving Gospel to the sad, decadent character in the drama called *The Princess*. Waking up in a strange hotel bedroom after an orgiastic night with a young gigolo, she stands looking out the window at the beach. She says: "Yes, I see that. And a strip of beach with some bathers, and then—an infinite stretch of nothing but water and—" She breaks off, crying out softly and turning away from the window. The young man she is with asks her, "What's the matter?" She replies, "Oh, God, I remember the thing I wanted not to! The goddam end of my life!" She draws a deep, shuddering breath. "Help me back to the bed! Oh, God, no wonder I didn't want to remember! I was no fool!"[2] Why is the good news of God sad for so many persons, tragic, enveloped in lostness and "might have been"?

This condition adds to the complexity and urgency of our task in the breakthrough for the Gospel, cutting through mental blocks and psychological hazards. "Take, eat, this is my Body, which is given for you. . . ." "Drink ye all of this; for this is my Blood of the New Testament, which is shed for you, and for many, for the remission of sins. . . ." How can we make this real, *relevant*—for any of the Angry Young Men ("no beliefs, no convictions, no enthusiasm")—for all the Princesses everywhere ("Oh, God, I remember the thing I wanted not to!")—for everybody who has heard (but not comprehended) or comprehended a part of the Gospel (and feared, not accepting by faith the whole of the Gospel)—and who has turned away?

Only the basic, down-to-earth evangelism of the Christian life will suffice—*the evangelism of the life in Christ.* This cannot be a technique or a gimmick; it is a human life offered to Christ or it is not, and its intention must be clear. When a human life is so offered to Christ, and is in Christ, evangelism is taking place. This surmounts all the conferences, the seminars, the books, the speeches, the strategies about evangelism, for this is evangelism.

Christ wants nothing less of us than this.

We realize how shallow our definition of evangelism has been, when we are confronted by true evangelism itself. It is love where we have let ourselves hate; patience where we have allowed ourselves to be restless; hope where we have let ourselves sink into despair; joy where we have let ourselves be gripped by morbid sadness; bearing another's burdens (one mile, and another mile, and another mile, and another . . .) where we have become outraged because of seeming ingratitude or difficulty after bearing another's burden for a half mile or three-fourths of a mile and have angrily fled away; adoration of God where we have stingingly given God a few hurried minutes out of a busy day and have then relegated God to the basement of our thoughts and affections so that we might once again become absorbed in "adoration" of ourselves.

In our own time, there are some marvelous insights into the profoundest meaning of evangelism. For example, going through my mail the other day, I came across *The Open Door*, a mimeographed newsletter of St. Leonard's House in Chicago, the Episcopal Church center that provides a haven for men coming out of prison who need rehabilitation and a new chance. Father Taylor of St. Leonard's House wrote something in the newsletter that captures the meaning of the true imperative of evangelism. He writes:

The Church allows us to use the crucifix not only to remind us of the historical Passion of Christ but to show us what is happening now, not only in prisons and on battlefields but in our own lives, to each of us. Our Lord did not choose His Passion only to suffer it in His human nature, but to suffer it in the suffering of each one of His members through all ages, until the end of time. The pain felt as a result of a small injustice or an unkind word this morning is the pain of Christ Himself, totally rejected and totally helpless on the cross. It is for this reason that your support of St. Leonard's House (both by your prayer and by your contributions) is so very important. It enables you to participate in the comforting of Christ.[3]

The Rule of the French community of Taizé grasps the meaning of the true imperative of evangelism when it states: "You would narrow your comprehension of the Gospel if, because you feared to lose your life, you would keep it yourself. *If the grain does not die,* you cannot hope to see your person open up in the fullness of the Christian life. . . . Like Abraham you can advance in this way only by faith and not by sight, being assured always that he who will have lost his life on account of Christ will find it."

The Little Brothers of Jesus and the Little Sisters of Jesus are communities in the Roman Catholic Church that have grown out of the experience in discipleship of Fr. Charles de Foucauld. In one of his letters, Fr. de Foucauld stated the principle that is basic to the religious communities following in his footsteps:

Of all Our Lord's sayings in the Gospel, I can think of none that made a deeper impression on me or had a greater effect on my life than this: ". . . when you did it to one of the least of my brethren here, you did it to me" (Matthew 25:40). If one stops to think that these words came from Uncreated Truth, fell from the lips that said, "this is my Body . . . this is my Blood . . . ," how powerfully one feels drawn to seek and love Jesus in these "little ones"! Give yourself to your neighbor— that is the best way of advancing toward God.[4]

The first part of the definition of evangelism quoted at the beginning of our discussion stated: "Evangelism is making the Gospel known to those who do not know it, in hope that they may be turned to God in faith. . . ." We have been dealing with this first part of the definition of evangelism, but now we come to the second part of it: ". . . and making it [the Gospel] more effectively known to those who already live within the Church, that their faith may grow in clarity and strength." We who already live within the Church will become better evangelists only as our faith grows in clarity and strength. Consequently, the achievement of the goal outlined in the first part of the definition ("making the Gospel known to those who do not know it") is dependent upon the achievement of the goal outlined in the second part of the definition.

We who already live within the Church are constantly being evangelists *for* Christ or *against* Christ. If we harbor racial hatred and bitterness within our hearts, we are being evangelists of racial hate (and, horribly, we are doing *this* under the very banner of Christ whom we are denying by our hatred and bitterness). If we narrow our concept of the Gospel and do not relate it to the whole of life, we are being evangelists of a stultifying, narrow, letter-of-the-law religion that is not Christianity (yet we perpetuate *this* under the very banner of Christ whom we are denying by our legalism and "churchly self-love"). If we make of the Church, the

Body of Christ, a mere "nice" social club, divided up into unrelated and feuding sections, more interested in social prestige and a fast buck than the Way of the Cross and prophetic social witness, we are being evangelists of a manipulable, soft, and flabby religion that is not the hard, demanding, transforming Christian faith (yet we perpetuate *this* under the very banner of Christ whom we are denying by our selfishness, social conformity—indeed, by our faithlessness in the revealed Son of God whose life and ministry so obviously always stood for different standards and values).

"Take, eat, this is my Body, which is given for you. . . ." Jesus invites us to *communion with himself.* Always we will fail, as sinful men and women, to love and serve Jesus as he deserves; but, inasmuch as he invites us to *communion with himself,* doesn't it behoove us to recognize Jesus who issues the invitation? He is the Savior revealed in Holy Scripture. While there will probably always be different interpretations of his words and actions, there are many clear aspects of his revelation that objectively speak to all people in all times, which seem to impel understanding of the *kind* of person he was. He identified himself always with the poor and outcast. He loved and healed and transformed human lives. He shunned the use of power and human prestige. Always. He pointed everything away from his own glory and toward the Father's glory. He emptied himself in mercy, kindness, and patience. He was unsentimental and, when the occasion demanded it, hard-hitting in his insistence upon justice and truth.

At least, let us be honest enough to perceive the depth of our sinning *against* Christ—when we weigh our Christian witness as manifested in our Church life over against his own human life—instead of blindly refusing to acknowledge our sin against him and, even when caught and sinking in our sin, proudly maintaining that we are witnessing for Christ.

". . . This is my Blood of the New Testament, which is shed for you, and for many, for the remission of sins. . . ." We, who already live within the Church, are we caught up in the dynamic love of Christ so that this same love, flowing through us—visible in the transparency of true discipleship—is itself unfettered, dynamic evangelism? We, who already live within the Church—is our faith growing "in clarity and strength," or is the Church, for us, another institution we have to do with in our social life, *another* demand upon our money, *another* source of "fellowship" (along with Rotary or Kiwanis or Lions or P.T.A. or the Masonic Lodge or . . .), *another* drain upon our time and energies?

". . . This is my Body. . . ." ". . . This is my Blood. . . ." Is it, really, for us? Is it, then, the staff of life itself? Is it the first thing in life for us, or do we place dozens of things "first"? Is the Sacrament the means of dynamic renewal and power for our always weak, self-centered, sick selves, who are by the Sacrament enabled to be evangelists of Christ, or is it just the source of a headache on the first Sunday of the month when the eucharistic service is so very long, a "habit" we have never actually understood, a bore, something seemingly irrelevant to the guts and blood and bite of tough, everyday life? Is the power of the Risen Christ sovereign, active, and dynamic in our lives, enabling our faith to grow "in clarity and strength"—enabling us to manifest our love of God by growing in love of our neighbor—transforming our always naturally self-centered lives into instruments of God's incredible, simple, divine love emptying itself completely for the agony and suffering of people?

The depth and vigor of our evangelism will reflect itself in the answer we must honestly give to these questions.

The Way of the Cross lies open for any and all Christians

who desire to be such instruments of God's love—and, therefore, instruments of evangelism of Jesus Christ. *Jesus Caritas,* a publication of the Charles of Jesus (Père de Foucauld) Association (October 1958) prints an excerpt from Michel Quoist's *Prayers* that illuminates the experience of the Way of the Cross of all who, wishing to be evangelists of Christ, open themselves to the love of God in love of humankind:

> Lord, why did you tell me to love men, all my brothers?
> I have tried but now I come back, frightened, to you . . .
> Lord, I was so peaceful in my house, I had everything nicely
> arranged and I was quietly settled in.
> My house was all furnished and everything seemed all right.
> Alone, I was at peace with myself, sheltered from the wind,
> the rain and the mire.
> I could have remained whole and intact, shut up in my tower.
> But you found a crack in my defenses, Lord;
> You made me open my door just a bit,
> And like a cloudburst full in the face, the cries of men awoke me;
> Like a gust of wind, I was shaken by a friendship;
> Like a ray of sun peeping unexpectedly between the shutters,
> your grace had disturbed me . . . and I left my door ajar,
> incautious that I was.
> Now I am lost, Lord!
> Outside men were watching for me.
> I had not known they were so near; in that house, in that

street, in that office—my neighbor, my colleague, my
    friend.
As soon as I started to open the door, I saw them there
    with
their hands, their looks, their very souls stretching out,
waiting like beggars outside a church.
The first of them came in, Lord—there was still a little
    room
in my heart.
I let them come gladly, I would have cared for them,
    talked
to them, cheered them, these sheep of mine, my own lit-
    tle flock.
You would have been pleased, Lord, well served, duly
honored—neatly and politely.
It was all quite reasonable up till then . . .
But those that followed, Lord—I had not seen those
    others;
they had been hidden by the first ones.
There were more of these; they were more wretched,
    too, and
they came streaming in without waiting to be asked.
We had to move up and make room for one another in
    my house.
And now they have come from everywhere, wave after
    wave
of them, each new wave pushing and jostling the last.
They have come from everywhere, from every part of
    the city,
from the entire country, from the whole world,
    uncountable, unending.
They no longer come singly, but in groups, in lines, as if
mixed together, bound together, welded together like
    pieces of humanity.

They no longer come with empty hands but laden with
    heavy
luggage—the luggage of injustice, of rancor and hate,
the luggage of suffering and sin.
Behind them they trail the world, with all its tools,
    twisted
and rusty or too new and ill-adjusted, wrongly used.
Lord, they are getting in my way, taking all the room,
    hurting me!
They are too hungry—they are devouring all I had and
    me myself.
I can do nothing any more; the more they push in and
    the
more they push at the door, the wider the door opens . . .
O Lord! My door is breaking down!
I can't go on! It is too much for me! Life is not worth
    this!
What about my position?
What about my family?
And my peace of mind?
And my freedom?
And what about me?
Ah! Lord! Everything has been taken from me. I no
    longer even belong to myself.
There is no room for me in my own house.

Have no fear, says God, you have not lost all but gained
    all.
For while men were pouring into your house,
I, your Father,
I, your Lord,
Slipped in with them.[5]

V. The Intention of All Our Evangelism

Thy kingdom come. Thy will be done, On earth as it is in heaven. (From the Lord's Prayer, Book of Common Prayer, page 82)

This sums up the intention of all our evangelism. Always, as Christians, we are told by our Christ to pray (our actions are prayers too) that the Father's will shall be done on earth as it is in heaven.

Of course, we understand that the Realm of Heaven has already come into human life in Jesus Christ, although the world's resistance to Christ must be broken down, individual life by individual life, personal decision by personal decision, society by society, even church by church. Breaking down such resistance must never lead us, in our evangelism, to manipulate or use anybody—even for the sake of Jesus. Above all, he wishes us to come to him by and with our own free wills. There is often a very fine line between evangelism and exploitation, but that line must be clearly understood and rigorously observed. Evangelism ceases absolutely to be evangelism when it becomes exploitation. The two are altogether different in motivation. We never manipulate anybody into salvation; we try to show forth Christ to them, and he is their salvation (as our own).

If we try manipulating anybody into "accepting the Lord," we are using means quite opposite from means he ever employed. The Gospel stands in judgment upon the means used to communicate it. We end up by conveying a very distorted picture of Jesus to people when we try to manipulate them into "accepting" him. He wants to be loved with the whole heart, not "accepted" because of shallow press-agentry, callous manipulation, or fear. It is a peak of irony to employ means to bring people into the way of Christ when such means are good illustrations of what the way of Christ is not.

In the area of "evangelistic enterprises" one is dismayed and saddened to find how much self-styled evangelism is obviously corrupted by exploitation, both in motivation and technique. Yes, evangelistic efforts by Christians will always be corrupted by selfish motives (as will any human service we offer to God), but can this not be openly admitted and repented of? Must it instead be perpetuated in the pharisaism of self-righteousness? ("Talk about your own motives; my motives are clean and pure. I am nonprofit for Jesus and the government recognizes this. Things are black-and-white simple, and I happen to be pure white!")

The farce of much self-styled evangelism that is merely profit-motivated, expertly publicized "religious" exploitation has, quite naturally, made a large number of people outside the Church distrustful of all organized "religious" activities. It has weakened the Church's best evangelistic efforts because "sincerity" has come to mean more to the public than "truth," and often contrived "sincerity" wallops across a message to the public when "truth" without artifice is colder than a dead mackerel insofar as people are concerned.

"Thy kingdom come? Delay it, Lord, delay it! Religion is paying off too well right now for me. Lord, religion is hot! Hold back the Kingdom a little longer!" This might well be said by "religious hucksters" whose intention in "evangelism" is love of the dollar, creating a theocracy, and amassing political power. It is not only con-men types, with low tastes and gauche ways of expressing themselves, who are "religious hucksters." The ranks are swelled by lady types and *gentleman* types, too, who look down *their* elitist noses at con-men types (and may hustle twice as many dirty bucks). Religion is paying off for a lot of people, let's face it; and a sickeningly pietistic line and "sincere" approach is very much a part of the game. It is one of the more disturbing aspects of our mass culture.

Amid the ballyhooed religious revival in America, a number of important voices are being raised that decry the sterility and empty institutionalism of Christianity. These voices cannot be ignored. But can it be that apostasy—forsaking of deep Christian commitment—has actually flowered amid a religious revival that was good for business? Despite the publicized religious revival, the world is increasingly passing the Church by.

There are magazine articles about religion, movies about it; there is personal "witnessing" in public; there is even a plethora of religious symbols in commercial advertising and promotion. There is a climate of religiosity that serves to dull numerous potentially sharp issues. There is a "religious" attitude that one hears expressed something like this: "Wonderful! God got his Name in the newspaper again!" "Great! Religion is really reviving. We landed another 15-minute program about religion on the radio!" "Did you see that big ad in all the magazines? They used a picture of a church in it! What progress for Christ!" Is it possible that this represents a massive sellout (on a Macy-Gimbel scale, with parades and balloons) to what culture can tangibly give to religion—with a resulting failure by the Church to persist in giving culture the sharp cutting edge of the Gospel?

There is a record amount of talk and publicity about religion, but one searches for the Christian style of life in much the same way as Diogenes walked through the streets of Athens looking for an honest man. There is an element of fashion in much contemporary American religiosity, but one is dismayed when confronted by the non-Christian social attitudes of a majority of professed and nominal Christians. The gospel of culture seems to be stronger within the Church than the Gospel of Christ.

One example of this may be found in the collusion of Christian apostasy with self-righteous American apostasy. "In God we trust," America proclaims to the rest of the world. Yet everybody knows (and we know, too) that America's trust is, like that of other nations, in weapons of war, industrial might, cultural imperialism, and dollars. Must the trappings of organized religion be brought out of the sanctuary of holy God to lend distorted credence to a spectacle of Mammon-worship? Does religion draw the line nowhere at what sins it will cloak? (But what if drawing the line should mean persecution of religion instead of fattening of religion? What then?) Is God mocked?

The weakening of the *intention* of Christian evangelism ("Thy kingdom come. Thy will be done, On earth as it is in heaven") is evident to a growing number of concerned and astute observers. Adlai Stevenson, writing in *Saturday Review,* noted:

> It is a painful fact that the Communists show a world-wide concern, which is largely lacking among the men of the West; the whole human race is their horizon. Their "brotherhood" is materialist, collectivist, athe-

ist, and we dislike it, but it embraces everybody, and it is the framework of policies that takes the missionaries of their new order to the ends of the earth. We have no corresponding commitment to our fellowmen. For hundreds of years, we have preached the Christian promise of brotherhood, but today, when vanishing space and scientific revolution have turned our planet into a single neighborhood, the ideal means little in terms of concern or conviction, in terms of policy or action.[1]

Similarly noting the lack of relationship between professed faith and relevant action in our Judeo-Christian culture, Paul Bowles (writing about the Muslims in *Holiday*, April 1959) compares Islam with Judaism and Christianity and reaches the following conclusion:

Islam, perhaps because it is the most recently born, operates the most directly and with the greatest strength upon the daily actions of those who embrace it. For a person born into a culture where religion has long ago become a thing quite separate from daily life, it is a startling experience to find himself suddenly in the midst of a culture where there is a minimum of discrepancy between dogma and natural behavior, and this is one of the great fascinations of being in North Africa.[2]

An eminent Christian has said, "Science is at its peak, while the Church has become a symbol of the good and the respectable, rather than a reality. It has grown dull and moralistic." The speaker is the Rev. William G. Pollard, priest-in-charge of St. Francis' Episcopal Church in Norris, Tennessee, and executive director of the Institute of Nuclear Studies at Oak Ridge. Religious News Service (January 1959) reported his comments made before a meeting at Albany's Cathedral of All Saints.

A number of sensitive, thinking men and women are rejecting membership in the Church. One realizes, certainly, that a large number of them are aware of the costliness of embracing Christianity (the costliness of sacrificing one's own will and way of doing things, and taking up Christ's instead) and turn away for that reason. But there are other reasons that have roots in our evangelistic failures. Many persons find the Church life as shown to them not related to the problems of everyday life as they have known life, and it is relevance they seek. Many turn away because they find the special language system of the Church too foreign, and no one will interpret it for them. Many naively look upon the Church as an institution that somehow seized exclusive rights on the simple Jesus and made him complicated—and no one will set them right on this. Many reject the Church because it is "only another social organization" (there are always extremes here, for the Church is, for such people, either "the best" or "the worst" social organization). Many turn away because all the Church seems to be doing is leveling negatives at society like cannon balls.

Yes, I realize that the people rejecting Church membership for such reasons are wrong because they have oversimplified complex factors and been guilty of accepting generalizations about the Church rather than digging for the truth. However, so is our evangelism wrong when many people who are sensitive and thinking go on rejecting the Church for the wrong reasons.

Evangelism requires being still and listening perhaps even more than it requires making speeches, writing books, and delivering sermons. We must listen to the world in order to find any point of contact at all with it. We have to listen in order to understand what questions are being asked, needs expressed, longings covered up by layer after layer of a lifetime of self-protection from exposure. Dwight Macdonald (writing in *Esquire,* March 1959) states a common condition that takes patient and trained listening to capture the sound thereof, for its disguises are legion: "Our special American sort of agony, the horror of aloneness . . ."

The reality of people: is the Church conscious enough of it? One wonders if it is possible to be conscious enough of this in our large congregations, and with the problem made more complicated by the masks people pass around, as if in a perpetual Mardi Gras, to disguise reality.

There is a woman who occasionally comes to a church; she has visited with the priest a few times on a casual basis; she knows some of the parish women because she has met them at bazaars and teas. Within her life there has been a shaking of foundations that was devastating to her. All her values seemed to be shifting kaleidoscopically. There seemed to be no central point of truth or hope. It never occurred to her to try relating all this to her Confirmation ("so long ago!") or to the Holy Eucharist ("I'm afraid I don't see what connection that could really have"). But apparently no one knows anything about the revolution that has been going on in her inner life, and, outwardly, she has seemed the same as usual. ("Isn't Mrs. Chadwick such a *happy* woman? Always smiling and laughing. It does me good just to have her around.")

The Church's evangelism has not yet been able to penetrate Mrs. Chadwick's life. Is the Church's failure precisely its failure to *know* Mrs. Chadwick? Has evangelism been seen too much as being on a departmental, organized, technique basis instead of being Christian personal relations?

Has Mrs. Chadwick had to "keep face" and put on as much of a "social front" at church, when she made her communion, as at her bridge club?

A preacher is standing in a pulpit. Faces are upturned to him, the church is still except for his speaking. What is really happening? Are minds racing away from him or are they joined with his? Are people receptive to the answer he may be giving, or are they furiously throwing nonverbal questions at him, one after another, chaotically and angrily? One parishioner, looking particularly intent, is preparing her shopping list for a church supper Thursday night. The young man—over there, in that pew—is deciding whether he will change his job tomorrow. One person—yes, that contented woman in the third row on the right side, who is *always* such a good listener and quite a saint in her quiet adjustment to life—perhaps she fits this description by Elizabeth Bowen in *The House in Paris:*

> Wherever she had lived, her life had been full of people dropping in for a minute from somewhere else, or making her their somewhere else. No one asked her to understand, or wanted what happened to them to happen to her. Could she have wished to be trodden down in a riot, be a mark for anger, or go down on a helpless abandoned ship?[3]

Conceivably, the woman sitting about half way back in church—looking particularly at peace this morning, refreshed, dressed in a bright spring outfit—conceivably she fits this description by Simone de Beauvoir in *The Mandarins:*

> I was imprisoned in that moment, bound hand and foot, an iron collar around my neck. The weight of my

body was stifling me, my breath was poisoning the
air. It was myself whom I wanted to escape, and it
was that, precisely, which would never be granted me
again.[4]

The elderly gentleman sitting over to the left—see? Now
he's looking down at his feet, he seems to be taking in every
word of the sermon today as if it had personal meaning for
him—could he be going over in his mind what he must say
to his daughter this afternoon? Could his thoughts run
something like the words spoken by the father to his daughter in James Agee's *A Death in the Family?*

I know it's unmitigated tommyrot to try to say a word
about it. To say nothing of brass. All I want is to warn
you that a lot worse is yet to come than you can imag-
ine yet, so for God's sake brace yourself for it and try
to hold yourself together. . . . It`s a kind of test, Mary,
and it's the only kind that amounts to anything. When
something rotten like this happens. Then you have
your choice. You start to really be alive, or you start to
die. That's all.[5]

Our evangelism, preaching, witnessing—all of it is often
not taking place in creative, meaningful dialogue, but in
something spewed out in a monologue that, if it strikes any
response at all, only evokes an overlapping monologue in
return.

Why?

A partial answer may be found in the intention of our
evangelism, preaching, and witnessing. If we simply want
the woman in the third row—see? over there, on the right
side—for her sizable church pledge and the social influence
she may wield in the community for our parish, our inten-

tion in bringing her into the church is sadly lacking. (In fact, if we refrain from preaching on a most important social issue because it might possibly offend this influential woman and thereby lead to a diminishing of our Church's prestige in certain important quarters of the community, our evangelism is doubly sadly lacking.)

If we simply want the woman sitting about half way back in church—yes, that's right, she's the one in the bright spring outfit—for her organizational skill and because she has three children nearing the age of Confirmation (and we want a big Confirmation class next fall), our intention in bringing her into the Church is sadly lacking.

The elderly gentleman sitting over there on the left? Well, our evangelism is sadly lacking unless we want him in the Church, too, for the basic reason, "Thy kingdom come. Thy will be done, On earth as it is in heaven." When the *intention* of our evangelism is right, then we are more concerned with people as persons, as children of God, as fellow pilgrims on our mutual way to fulfillment in God's will. Our real concern communicates itself, if not instantly and electrically, then patiently and steadily. It becomes a strong foundation, for it is the foundation of Christ's own concern.

In all that we do, as Christians, it is God's will that we pray may be realized—in human relations of all kinds, in all marriages and relationships, in all families, in all racial relations, in all educational institutions, in all the arts, in all businesses, in all labor organizations.

Even though we face painful crucifixion of our own wills and desires, worship of tradition, and future plans, we pray: "Thy kingdom come. Thy will be done, On earth as it is in heaven." We have brought to Christ sins and failures, individually and socially, and left them with him. Now, in confidence, we utter this petition of the Lord's Prayer. It is the motor of our evangelism that keeps running, when we ourselves are tired and might momentarily like to stop and sleep. "Thy kingdom come. Thy will be done. . . ." And so we go on, renewed, in the footsteps of Christ.

VI. The Image of Our Evangelism

And here we offer and present unto thee, O Lord, our selves, our souls and bodies, to be a reasonable, holy, and living sacrifice unto thee. .... (From the final paragraph of the Prayer of Consecration, Book of Common Prayer, page 81)

Our response to God, or our lack of response to God, goes to make up the "image" (or concept or picture) of the Church that other people have.

People have an image of just about everything: a brand of cigarettes, an automobile, a political figure, a Hollywood star, a deodorant, a major Church denomination, a local parish, a local department store, a newspaper. When any of these is mentioned, immediately an image of some sort comes to the minds of most people. It is a good or bad image, generally speaking. It may well be the sort of image the institution or individual would like other people to have, but it may also be exactly the opposite sort of image of the one desired.

These days one hears a good deal, in certain Church circles, about "the image of the Church." What is meant, simply, is, "What do other people really think of the Church?"

This does not necessarily refer to what other people consciously believe they think of the Church; it has to do with what they *actually* (even subconsciously) think about the Church.

Our response, as members of the Church, to God's will and purpose basically determines what other people actually think about the Church—for despite the prosperity, prestige, and power that a church may represent in a community, its image (if it is a desirable one) will be largely based on whether or not it stands for truth rather than expediency, the sense of the holiness of God and the relevance of this holiness to people's everyday lives that it is able to communicate, and if it reveals unswerving courage in speaking God's Word to the society in which it dwells. Many people will always bend the knee publicly to power—and consciously respect it, too—but actually will hold it in contempt if it is refuting by outward manifestation what it inwardly is meant to be. An example of this is found in *The Glitter and the Gold,* the memoir of Consuelo Vanderbilt Balsan, who, as a young English duchess, had visited the Austrian imperial court of Franz Joseph. She had witnessed the annual Maundy Thursday observance of the "foot washing," a tradition based upon our Lord's washing of the disciples' feet. At the imperial court, the Emperor each year washed the feet of twelve beggars. Mrs. Balsan wrote of the event:

> Originally intended as an act of humility, it had become, when I saw it, a scene of splendor in which arrogance masqueraded in spurious simplicity. Twelve of the oldest and poorest men in Vienna were seated on a bench just in front of the tribune from which I watched the scene. They had been carefully washed and scented so that no unpleasant odor should offend

the Imperial nostrils. I was told that on one occasion
such precautions had been neglected and that the Emperor at the time had been nearly overcome as he knelt
to wash the filthy feet extended to him. The feet now
were faultlessly clean—one might almost say mani-
cured—and each man in turn placed a foot in per-
fumed water. When the Emperor reached the last man
he raised his weary eyes in which I saw disillusion
shine cold and bleak. Then rising he returned to the
archdukes, who were dressed in gorgeous uniforms
and stood in line facing us. . . . It saddened me that an
act of Christian humility such as the washing of the
beggars' feet should have become an operatic scene
shorn of all spiritual meaning.[1]

The desired image of the event of the Emperor's washing
the feet of twelve beggars and the actual image of the event
were, we realize, in sharp contradiction to each other. How
often this situation is so, in many aspects of life—including
contemporary Church life. The only way to go about correcting a bad image of anything is, first, to try finding out
what people's actual image *is* of an institution or person or
practice. Then, one must go about changing the image—if it
is unlike the desired image—*by correcting the fault in the actual situation that, in turn, has given rise to the undesirable
image.*

For example, if a parish has a community image depict-
ing it as a "snob" parish—and if it does not desire this (may
God help it, if it does)—the first thing it must do is to
change what actual conditions have led to its being known
as a "snob" parish. If the parish were to call in a top-drawer
public relations agency to change its image, but were not to
change the actual conditions that had given rise to its repu-
tation in the community for snobbishness, this would

merely be a short-range solution that would ultimately backfire. The only long-range solution would be honest diagnosis, honest surgery—and then, if it were considered expedient, a public relations campaign might be carried out within the community to make known the parish's actual post-operative condition.

Finding out about faulty images is a wonderful thing for the Church to do because, in changing faulty images about ourselves, we often correct basic faults in ourselves. The Church is as much called to honest self-examination before Christ as the individual Christian is called. The images of the Church's life and action that are bad ones—and, in the Church's own eyes, undesirable ones—have generally come into being because the oblation of the Church to God has been weak or insincere. A penitent and most acceptable use of a bad image of some phase of the Church's life and actions is our letting the image be a mirror. Of course, we can angrily reject the image, denouncing those who hold it and rationalizing away their reasons for doing so. Or, to our credit and faithfulness, we may accept the existence of the image as true, acknowledging that it rightly reflects a fault we have not had the courage heretofore to face squarely or to try to correct. Valid and effective evangelism cannot fail to grow out of such honesty.

If we want to find out the truth about ourselves, we can learn immensely important and profitable things by ascertaining what is the image of our church held by other people, both Christians and non-Christians. It is conceivable that a parish that considers itself traditionally to be "Evangelical" may be revealed, in its community image, as being unbearably stiff, rigid, inflexible, and closed in upon itself in a social sense that automatically would hinder Evangelical outreach. It is conceivable that a parish that considers itself traditionally to be "Catholic" may be revealed, in its community image, as being unbearably parochial, self-righteous, defensive, obsessed with paraphernalia, and likewise closed in upon itself in a sense that automatically would hinder Catholic outreach.

Or, a parish that considers itself to be vitally interested in social justice may be revealed, in its community image, to be interested academically in social justice but actually more concerned with talking and meeting about such problems than really doing anything sacrificial about them. A parish that considers itself to be speaking articulately to the community in a prophetic way about the sicknesses and failures of the community to be Christian may be revealed, in its community image, to be failing to reach "point of contact" with the community at all—with the result that all the articulate, prophetic speaking, is falling on deaf ears. A parish that considers itself to be laying down its life for the preservation of vital traditions may be revealed, in its community image, to be concerned with fossilized rather than living traditions and, in fact, to be encased in a museum rather than a church. A parish that considers itself to be *avant-garde* in a most exciting and provocative way, always doing new things that cry out to be done and providing the whole community with a stimulating and contemporary proclamation of the Gospel, may be revealed, in its community image, to be exceedingly eccentric and, as a matter of fact, mumbling gobbledygook.

What is the community image of the peak moments in the life of a parish?

It is Christmas. The altar is decked with flowers, the church well heated, the building packed with people (who have just opened, or will soon open, a king's ransom in yuletide presents). Is the parish revealed, in the community image, to be thankful for the birth of the Son of God into human life, or for the richness of yuletide presents, the good life, national supremacy, and the security of yet another year's solid status quo of life? Is the parish revealed, in the community image, to be thankful because the Incarnation is for the "nice" people (themselves), the socially acceptable, the Americans and the whites and the nominal, self-styled Christians—or to be thankful because the Incarnation is also for "the blind . . . the lame . . . the lepers . . . the deaf . . . the dead . . . the poor . . ." (themselves), the "bad" people, the socially unacceptable, the non-Americans, the nonwhites, the honestly self-styled agnostics. . . ? What is the *reality* underlying the community image of the parish?

It is Easter. Is the parish revealed, in the community image, to be sharing joyfully with the Risen Christ in his victory over sin and death or, instead, to have barred the church door to keep Jesus Christ outside because it knows the cost to its "security" and ways of doing things if it should let him enter in? Is the parish revealed, in the community image, to be trying to enter into meaningful solidarity of prayer and sacrifice with other Christians in the world suffering under totalitarian persecution who, because of their witness to Christ, are in danger of losing their jobs and homes, of being imprisoned, denied education and advancement, feeling extreme physical hunger and even facing death—or to be anxious only to get straight home to a dinner table heaped with food and decorated by chocolate Easter bunnies? What is the *reality* underlying the community image of the parish?

The image of the Church reflects in many ways the sincerity and depth of the Church's oblation and thanksgiving to God. Evangelism is making the Gospel known to people; it is not revivalism to awaken faith in one's self or one's nation, in "the Religion of the American Way of Life," in scientific progress or cultural values. Because evangelism has been misunderstood and often distorted, such revivalism has given rise to a significant apostasy in the very midst of America's highly touted religious revival. Instead of holy God, people have been confronted by a utilitarian deity who wins football games, puts America first—right or wrong—and dispenses a magical elixir to rid individuals of all their troubles.

"This is no time for remoteness or for lulling slogans or for the avoidance of hard truths," Edward Weeks wrote in *The Atlantic*. One can only say "amen" to this. The proclamation of the saving Gospel to the whole condition of humankind, to the whole condition of society, cannot be stifled, rationalized, secured inside the ghetto of "religion," and defeated by complacently nominal Christians who wish to keep the risen and glorified Christ at bay. "Church-as-usual" cannot be perpetuated. Unawakened churches cannot remain unable to meet the deep crisis experienced by people in this age (a crisis of which unawakened churches sadly seem to be unaware). The Gospel cannot be bottled up in sealed jars of sweet-smelling false piety. Matters of second- and third-rate importance in Christian living cannot be given smug precedence over life-and-death matters of first-rate significance: the self-contradictions implicit in much Church life cannot simply be glossed over as if they did not exist.

The conversion of the Church by culture is resulting in a watered-down, nonrecognizable caricature of the faith that meets certain pragmatic needs growing out of selfish preoccupation but fails to assert the demands of holy God. Much of our Church life becomes a syncretistic haze labeled "Christian" and perpetuated by laziness or indifference or ignorance. The Christian faith needs radical, unsentimentalized, brave, clear *showing forth*. Even a very small number of Christians, if committed to discipleship to

Christ, may be effective stewards and evangelists of the Gospel amid our profound crisis in communication.

Listen, Church! Listen, World!

An incredibly wide gulf separates the tight little island that is the life and world of an average parish church from the effective proclamation of the saving Gospel to the whole condition of humankind and the whole condition of society. *Yet the Gospel must be communicated to the parish in order that the parish may communicate the Gospel to the world!*

How can the gulf be bridged? This problem cannot be solved simply by ecclesiastical summit conferences or by Church leaders alone. It will come to be solved only as the bastion of a parish (one, then another and another) *abandons isolationism* and *accepts coexistence* with the Church at large.

Communicating the Gospel to the parish in an effective way is made difficult by the fact that only a tiny minority is really prepared to receive the Gospel, while a majority of the parish *thinks* it is prepared to receive it and certainly thinks it wants to receive it. Our church-urbanism has to be looked at in a clear light; ours is not privilege so much as it is responsibility. Responsibility to whom? "Thou shalt love the Lord thy God. . . . Thou shalt love thy neighbor as thyself. . . ."

It is too easy to generalize about the great issues challenging the whole Church while refusing to be specific about issues facing the parish. What are we, as a parish, doing in regard to these issues? There are several contemporary key issues, yet they all come together in one key issue facing the Church everywhere and in each parish: The loss of the vocation of ministry by the individual Christian and the individual parish.

When the individual Christian or parish acts responsibly

in relation to any of the key issues confronting the Church in our time, the Gospel has been communicated. There has taken place real evangelism. Because of the loss of the vocation of ministry by the individual Christian and parish, the identity of Christian action has largely disappeared. Christian action nowadays is associated in the popular mind with quite overt "religious" action—this stemming from mass cultural concepts. An identifiable Christian style of life, individually and socially, is largely missing from the contemporary scene. The salt has lost more of its savor than will generally be admitted.

Have individual Christians comprehended that they have a *ministry* to perform, whether they are clergy or lay? Have they grasped the meaning of the parish as being the whole people of God, *in this particular place,* and of their own distinctive roles within the Body of Christ?

Have they witnessed to the faith by showing it forth (mostly nonverbally and unself-righteously) in whatever area of "the world" they happen to be occupying?

Has the parish been a mediating force of grace, a dynamic centrifugal force of Christian education and enlightenment, a channel of divine love pouring into the neighborhood? If not, does it have a sin to confess—socially, publicly, repentantly? (But what if it feels no guilt?) "What is the will of the Lord?" is the question asked by a radical Christian ministry in any age. In the face of the answer to that question, all things must be prepared to be swept away that impede the realization *here, now,* of God's will. This will rock the parish to its foundations for, ironically, it is among the most conservative of all bodies in our society. Conservative, while paying lip-service to the revolutionary Jesus Christ who is always the transformer of life, individual and social, changing it from self-love into surrender to God's absolute love ethic.

Take the racial problem confronting the world Church. It can be solved at the local level only by the parish relating vocation to action. Increasingly, it seems to me that racism is the point upon which we stand or fall as followers of Jesus Christ in this generation. To a small Midwestern parish Africa seems so remote. Many American men and women may sincerely give their time to reading about Christian witness in Africa, but they are not yet prepared to relate it to *themselves*. They are often blind when it comes to seeing that the racial crisis is not just writ large on another continent, but is writ large *here* in this community *now*.

I came upon a small white boy in the interracial neighborhood of my Midwestern parish jabbing a pocketknife into a wooden pole. "I wish it was a nigger," he said. On another occasion I stood with some one hundred youngsters, mostly African Americans with a scattering of whites, and listened as a white boy shouted to a black social worker: "Dirty black nigger, dirty black nigger . . ." until a bus arrived to take the youngsters for a summer day's outing under parish auspices. Racial hatred, ingrained by environment as much as heredity, is there. The cross atop the parish church literally casts a shadow upon the tragic, ironical life scenes of hate and revenge.

The only salvation for such life-scenes in the neighborhood of a parish church is to be found in an identifiable Christian style of life, growing out of a recovered vocation of Christian ministry and manifested in love, writ small and applied quite specifically and sacrificially. (Is 11:00 a.m. on Sunday morning in *this* parish the most segregated hour in the week within the neighborhood?) Why prate about the Cross if one will not walk in the Way of the Cross, *here, now?* Why spin strategies for other continents if one will not accept the hard imperative of such strategies *here, now?* Why perpetuate, at great expense of energy and agony, the institution of the Church if one believes it to be essentially an expendable social organization (albeit at the highest level of human altruism) and not a holy people called into being by God, redeemed and ruled by Jesus Christ, indwelt by the Holy Spirit, and commanded to proclaim the Gospel to all the world?

A parish is a family for which Christ was content to be betrayed and given up into the hands of the wicked, and to suffer death upon the Cross. But Christ did not just die, he died to *save* the world; and he rose from the dead. The family that is a parish must be content too to die—unto its own will, its own ways, its own self-centeredness—if it is really to proclaim salvation unto the other people, outside the parish, for whom Christ also died. Only by being content to enter into such death can the parish experience that resurrection that manifests itself in renewed vocation. Such new life is essential if the parish is to be vital, dynamic, Christ-centered, prophetic, sacrificial, *if, in fact, it is to be the Church.*

The Gospel lacks meaning or purpose without the world. The Church needs the world to ask the honest, realistic questions that it is holding within itself. The Church needs the world to accept the Church, *here, now,* not waiting for perfection to come in it, but loving it for its divine calling and human condition.

The world needs the Church and is imperfect unless it is related to the Church, as the Church needs the world and is imperfect unless it is related to the world. The world needs the Church and not a sociological caricature of the Church that is simply a nice place to go, a place where a flame of religious belief is perpetually burning as a museum piece or "memorial" to a dead event. The world needs the Church and the hard, saving Gospel of Christ instead of "cheap grace," which is unreal grace.

The world must learn not to leave the Church when it encounters unreality. The Church is the one place where the world can honestly expect to be confronted by reality. The world must demand it of the Church. The Church cannot refuse it, for the Church is not its own; it is the Body of Christ.

VII. The "How" of Our Evangelism

*Almighty and everliving God, we most heartily thank thee
... that we are very members incorporate in the mystical
body of thy Son, which is the blessed company of all faithful people; and are also heirs through hope of thy everlast-
ing kingdom, by the merits of his most precious death and
passion....* (From Post-Communion Thanksgiving,
Book of Common Prayer, page 83)

The "how" of our evangelism is to be found in our response
to the love of God by offering ourselves in thanksgiving to
be used by God. The techniques we need to employ in the
"how" of our evangelism will grow out of our essential ac-
ceptance of *involvement* in God's purpose and *solidarity* in
the condition of our fellow human beings.

Of course, God has to enable our response to love, for
such response is alien to our innate and well-cultivated self-
love, which wars furiously against God's calling us to love
God instead.

We live today not only in "the Age of Publicity" but in a
vortex of hidden persuasion of "hard" and "soft" sell and
untold gimmicks that are aimed to influence the making of
decisions. The cold fact that we are living in a mass culture

was underlined by the following Associated Press dispatch from Long Beach, California:

> Mrs. Virginia Smith delivered her own baby without help while watching television from a couch in her living room.
>
> "It was a good movie and I didn't want to turn it off," Mrs. Smith, 38 years old, explained yesterday.
>
> Mrs. Smith's husband, James, a carpenter, had gone to bed in the next room three hours earlier. She roused him in time to help her snip the umbilical cord with a pair of sewing scissors.

Even selling Bibles can be more salesmanship than evangelism in our mass culture. Martin Mayer, in his book *Madison Avenue, U.S.A.* tells how advertising executive Stanley Resor earned money during his Yale vacations by selling Bibles door to door. "No better experience for an advertising man could be imagined, because the people who buy Bibles already own Bibles; to sell them another one is an exercise in pure salesmanship."[1]

Religion is making news in a bigger way than it ever did before. Religion is prominently represented on the lists of best-selling books and religious subjects are featured increasingly in mass-selling magazines. MUSIC BUSINESS GETS RELIGION was a banner headline across *Variety*. Hollywood has found that religion pays off at the box office: *A Man Called Peter* was the second largest grosser among films in 1955 and *The Ten Commandments* set a global box-office record.

Much "religion" in the mass media is exploitation of religion for financial-prestige reasons. How can we utilize the mass media—the press, television, radio, motion pictures, magazines—for the extension of valid Christian evangelism?

I would like to offer several concrete suggestions.

First, we should urge the mass media not to lose their critical faculty. It is easy to reflect the popular attitude toward the Church, which is one of indulgence. Often the mass media are content simply to promote what the Church wants promoted. This hurts the Church very badly, though it seems not yet to realize it. The mass media—particularly the press—"smell" news in politics, foreign affairs, the arts, and business, but frequently abdicate this function when they deal with religion. As a direct result, reporting of religious news is often exceedingly dull. This is one important reason why religious news is not widely read. Frequently church handout publicity blurbs are printed verbatim on Church pages. One finds lacking a sense of "news." Instead, a Church page often ironically reflects a weekly unseen battle for denominational balance. Who can blame a Church page editor? It is not an editor's fault, but that of the churches.

Second, the mass media—especially television and motion pictures—should be urged by the Church to avoid the mass media stereotypes that are so increasingly evident. Priests, ministers, and rabbis are relegated completely out of reality, in many cases of dramatic portrayal, because *nobody* is that "nice." Also most clergy are not, actually, able to compete in studied charm and physical attraction with attractive young actors and actresses just out of dramatic school or established stars—but these performers portray the majority of clergy on television and in films. As a matter of fact—speaking of mass media stereotypes—most clergy do not go about wearing studied expressions that convey an immediate and arresting impression of "sincerity"—yet they are wearyingly often so portrayed in the mass media. Clergy, in fact, are like other people, partly good, partly bad—as anyone knows who is a churchgoer. Of course, churchgoers take a drubbing in conformity from the mass media, too. "Church people aren't *like* other people," one might say after seeing church life portrayed in mass media. (Yet they *are*, they are human, and it is most important to emphasize this.)

Third, mass media personnel who are given religious assignments need to know basic Christian theology and doctrine. (This may be somewhat akin to the value of a Berlitz course for a person who will be going to France or Germany to represent a United States firm there.) What is the Christian belief about creation, sin, the nature of God? It is imperative for communications workers to be acquainted with basic tenets of the faith they are writing or speaking about, and interpreting. A television station or a newspaper will often send a staff member, lacking rudimentary religious instruction, to cover a news event such as a Church convention or conference, yet the same station or newspaper would not consider sending an unqualified person to cover a political or musical event of comparable importance. Because of a lack of rudimentary religious instruction, clergy are frequently quoted out of context in a way that seriously distorts the meaning of what they really said.

To go a step further: mass media personnel must seriously receive some indoctrination about the jungle of Christian denominationalism if they are going to report or interpret religion intelligently. The Protestant-Catholic-Jewish structure of American Church life is a gross oversimplification. For example, Islam is experiencing rapid growth. A number of other Christians are offended by the Roman Catholic use of the word "Catholic," believing that it applies equally to themselves, even though they are not *Roman* Catholic. Christian Scientists are not Protestants. Orthodox Church members are neither "Catholic" nor "Protestant." Mormons do not fit into any one of the three classic (Protestant-

Catholic-Jewish) classifications. In publicity material distributed by the World Council of Churches, three non-Roman Catholic member bodies are sharply differentiated: Protestant, Orthodox, and Anglican.

In the denominational jungle, Christian traditions and customs radically differ from one church to another. For example, a Protestant church in a leading American city, one recalls, claims that Baptism is not necessary for church membership but nonetheless provides—if desired—Baptism by immersion or sprinkling. It is our clear responsibility, as Christians and Church spokespersons, to provide Christian teaching to persons in the mass media who cover religion. It is equally our clear responsibility, as Christians and Church spokespersons, to seek instruction about the mass media of our times, so that we may understand the workings and underlying principles of television, motion pictures, radio, the press, magazines, advertising, and public relations.

Fourth, we should strive to help the mass media to relate religion to the rest of the human life that they are reporting and interpreting. At present, religion remains an isolated segment of the news (with the exception of a momentous news event concerning religion, a church scandal, or news coverage of a church celebrity). It seems to be a major part of our task to instill something of the meaning of the Church in the minds of the mass media personnel assigned to religion. (This now takes place at a broadcast network or major metropolitan newspaper level, but seldom below it.) The Church is more than a cluttered group of metropolitan churches: there is a historical perspective in which it needs to be seen, in order to be understood.

Fifth, we can take the lead in the whole field of communications (of which we are certainly an integral part) to seek a redefinition of what constitutes a "message." Often the

Church is looked at askance by mass media because it seems to be trying to "preach" or to get across a "message." Yet the same mass media will welcome with open arms the news of Washington, Hollywood, business, labor, and the arts. Always, in any field of news and interpretation, there is a "message." Every popular song, film, television or radio show, magazine, comic strip, or newspaper is disseminating "messages" by molding the thought and action patterns of men, women, and children. In our society, there is an appalling ignorance of what constitutes a "message." It is important to us, as members of a mass culture, that we stick hard to the task of redefining a "message." If we do, we may halt either a political demagogue or the hideous conformity that a mass culture implicitly "preaches" constantly.

Various Church people are commencing to wrestle with some of the major problems confronting the Church as it exists in mass culture. In my book *Crisis in Communication*— particularly in the chapter entitled "The Age of Publicity"— I have attempted to state some of these problems. William Lynch, S.J., engages in a discussion of related problems in his book *The Image Industries*. Father Lynch conceives the following to be the four fundamental issues in the art of the mass media:

1. The failure, on a large scale, of these media to differentiate between fantasy and reality; the result is a weakening, throughout the nation's audiences, of the power to differentiate between these two things.
2. The weakening and flattening out of the area of feeling and sensibility in the public consciousness.
3. The extent to which freedom of imagination is being restricted, not by the moralist or the censor, but by the purveyors of all the techniques for the fixation of the imagination.

4. The "magnificent imagination": the spectacular projection of the dream on the screens of the movies and television, in which all the true lines of our human realities are lost.[2]

The "how" of our evangelism must take into account the correction of weaknesses in the mass media instead of exploitation of them. The techniques employed in the "how" of our evangelism must be techniques of valid evangelism, not mere gimmicks of religious huckstering. The dangers implicit in religious huckstering are manifold. For example, in a provocative book entitled *Battle for the Mind*,[3] William Sargant writes that "the techniques employed in religious conversions" often approximate so closely the modern political techniques of brainwashing and thought control that each throws light on the mechanics of the other.

In the absence of available clinical reports on the physiological changes noted in persons who have been subjected to intolerable mental stress in modern brainwashing, the author offers "parallel texts" of John Wesley's *Journal* in 1739 and Grinker and Spiegel's report on their treatment of acute war neuroses in North Africa in 1942. The author finds the main difference between these two accounts is "the philosophical explanations" given for "the same impressive results." Wesley attributed the phenomena to the intervention of the Holy Ghost, Grinker and Spiegel to a demonstration of the correctness of Freud's theories.

Dr. Sargant compares Wesley's reports of how he induced "almost identical states of emotional excitement" by his particular sort of preaching with the author's own work in a wartime neurosis center in England. With the help of Pavlov's findings, Dr. Sargant and his wartime colleagues evolved a technique of deliberately stimulating anger or fear, under drugs, until a patient would collapse in temporary emotional exhaustion. The fear of burning in hell—induced by Wesley's graphic preaching in the consciousness of his hearers—was compared by Dr. Sargant with the suggestion he might force on a returned soldier, during treatment, that he was in danger of being burned alive in his tank and must fight his way out.

The leaders of "successful faiths" have never dispensed entirely with "physiological weapons" in their evangelism, Dr. Sargant states. As some of the methods used to modify normal brain function for religious purposes, he cites the following: fasting, chastening of the flesh by scourging and physical discomfort, regulation of breathing, disclosure of awesome mysteries, drumming, dancing, singing, inducement of panic fear, weird and glorious lighting, incense, and intoxicant drugs. He says that "all the physiological mechanisms" exploited for the purpose of debilitation by Pavlov in his animal experiments "short of glandular change by castration, seem, in fact, to have been exploited by [Jonathan] Edwards or his successors in their Calvinist missionary campaigns." The author urges the Church's leaders "to take more advantage of the normal person's emotional mechanism for disrupting old behavior patterns and implanting new."

Dr. Sargant groups together "historical techniques of human indoctrination, religious conversion, brainwashing and the like" and, again, "politicians, priests, psychiatrists and police forces. . . ." At the end of the book, speaking of the methods he has discussed, Dr. Sargant writes: "If we are to promote true religion, preserve our democratic ways of life and our hard-won civil liberties, we must learn to recognize that these same methods are being used for trivial and evil purposes instead of noble purposes."

It is precisely at this point that I take the greatest exception to what he advocates; and I maintain that he is saying things that vitally concern us. If a technique or method is wrong, is it not better that it should be used for evil purposes than for noble purposes? It is a very hard question. Corrupt methods and noble purposes ought not to have any traffic with one another in a deliberate way; yet, actually, they will have a good deal of traffic with one another, in the natural course of events, because of the moral ambiguities that are found in "noble" and "evil" purposes alike. As Christians and evangelists, we must avoid all possible conscious and deliberate linking of corrupt methods with noble purposes. Surely, the very nature of Christian evangelism makes this demand upon our integrity.

One is asked the question: Is the Church supposed to employ techniques in its evangelism activity? And: Are techniques "wrong?" The "how" of our evangelism will always grow out of a combination of evangelistic motivation and the techniques that are both available for our use and sufficiently integrally related to our motivation and purpose.

At our local levels—as lay people and clergypersons living and working in particular communities and as members of individual parishes in particular communities—our evangelistic efforts may, and should, complement national Church evangelism, particularly that which utilizes the mass media of communication. However, this is only a beginning of local evangelism, not its fulfillment.

Local evangelism often grows out of a local need for evangelism. Canon Ernest W. Southcott, who is noted for his experiments with the "house-church" in England, did not originate a new method in a vacuum, but responded to a desperate need in his own community. How to reach the unchurched, the lapsed baptized, the lapsed communicants, the nonchurchgoing members of parish families? The "house-church" was the response in his parish to the need in that community. A carbon copy of the "house-church" in another parish—even if one carefully duplicated techniques right down the line—might be a blunder and failure. Why? Because it might not be a response to a need, but merely a gimmick, or something too casually superimposed upon a parish structure, thereby eliminating the factor of suffering pointing up need, and eliminating also sweat and initial strategy being formed in indigenous soil.

Storefront churches are found in various areas of the country for carrying on evangelism in particular neighborhoods. Downtown church centers and even chapels are being opened up in office buildings, providing an on-the-spot ministry for literally thousands of workers in dense business areas of cities.

Canon Theodore O. Wedel has spoken of the need to "gossip the Gospel." This can be a source of dynamic for evangelism in almost any local situation. Talk the Gospel of Christ! Talk it as much as one's own problems or Johnny's toothache or Sally's school prom or. . . . Talk the Gospel, gossip it, relate it to everyday life, brim over a bit with enthusiasm about it—because it is the good news of our salvation. Who ever heard good news like *that* before? There needs to be much more "gossiping the Gospel" at the local level not only to awaken interest in new Church members but to awaken enthusiasm and new life in old ones.

There is the crucial need to awaken the laity—at the local level—to the fact that they are the people of God, not just a once-a-week congregation making antiphonal responses in public worship. The Iona Community in Scotland and the Christian Faith and Life Community in Austin, Texas, have done groundbreaking work at local levels in this regard that has attracted worldwide interest and attention. So has the Zoë Movement in Greece carried on important work with the laity in arousing men and women of local parishes to Christian responsibility. *How are we to go about doing this?* By relating our Christian faith to our work, whatever it happens to be. By means of stewardship, so that giving to the Church is changed from a superficial monotonous "token payment" to an offering to Christ of *ourselves,* our time, and our work.

Local evangelism is in progress when a parish church or group of Christians takes a strong Christian stand on a social issue or exercises a leadership role of social responsibility in an area of community life marked by exploitation or injustice. In his book *A Time to Speak,* Michael Scott tells about a thorny crisis involving the British Government and several African leaders. Injustice was evident in the situation to many observers, including the author. He comments succinctly: "In all this the voice of Christian opinion seemed strangely muted."[4] How often this seems to be so! One can certainly strive to change this situation so that the voice of Christian opinion is not muted, but clearly heard, at the local level at which one lives.

Evangelism "writ small" takes place at the parish level, within the parish dimension. A parish ought not to look around for lists of ideas for evangelism, with the plan of checking off one idea, then another, until the ideal idea is found. A parish ought, instead, to examine itself honestly—its strongest values and its weakest points—and to examine the community in which it is situated. What are the most pressing needs within that particular community to which the parish might minister? In what quite definite ways—and for what quite definite reasons—is the parish not making a breakthrough into the life of that particular community or a given segment of it? What needs to be done to correct this situation? Indeed, what can be done?

The next step can be a program of local evangelism. It can not only serve to communicate the Gospel of Christ to unchurched persons in the community and to bring them into the Church; it can also stimulate, jolt, awaken, and inspire the local parish as nothing else can do.

"What about *me*? I'm just an individual on the local scene. How can I carry out the task of evangelism in my parish and community?"

First, by sincerely and repentantly trying to be a better Christian. Second, by recognizing that the "how" of "my evangelism"—as of all evangelism—is to be found in my response to the love of God by offering God *myself* in thanksgiving for God's inestimable gift to me, to us. Third, by finding specific application for evangelism in my own life, my own home, my own work, my own leisure. Do I accept evangelism yet as a full-time vocation, or do I still relegate it to certain times and certain occasions? This will make all the difference. Fourth, by doing my evangelism *in prayer*, in the realized presence of Jesus Christ with me. One should say, by *living in prayer*, in the realized presence of Jesus Christ with me; for "doing evangelism" and "living" are inseparable.

It is not only "the Church" that needs to focus all of its adoration and attention on God. Nor is it only "humankind" who needs to do this. It is I. When I focus my entire being, all of my adoration and attention, on God, then I am enabled too to bring myself into clear, sharp focus as a person created and redeemed by God.

In this focus, and as a result of it, *evangelism is taking place*.

Notes

CHAPTER I

1. Edmund Fuller, *Man in Modern Fiction*. New York, Random House, Inc., 1958.
2. Paul Elmen, *The Restoration of Meaning to Contemporary Life*. New York, Doubleday & Co., Inc., 1958.
3. Christopher Fry, *A Sleep of Prisoners*. New York, Oxford University Press, 1951.
4. Winthrop Sargeant in *The New Yorker*, November 8, 1958.

CHAPTER II

1. James A. Pike and W. Norman Pittenger, *The Faith of the Church*. Greenwich, Seabury Press, 1951.
2. I have written about these and other movements and experiments—Zoë in Greece, Iona in Scotland, and such works in Britain as the Christian Frontier Council, Cumberland Lodge, and St. Anne's House, Soho, in my book *Crisis in Communication* (New York, Doubleday & Co., Inc., 1957). Canon Ernest W. Southcott has written at length about the House-Church in his book *The Parish Comes Alive* (New York, Morehouse-Barlow Co., 1957). See also my review article about Canon Southcott's book entitled "One Way" in *The Christian Century*, February 10, 1957.
3. Malcolm Boyd, *Crisis in Communication*. New York, Doubleday & Co., Inc., 1957.

4. This idea is more fully developed in my book *Christ and Celebrity Gods* (Greenwich, Seabury Press, 1958).

CHAPTER IV

1. John Osborne, *Look Back in Anger.* New York, Criterion Books, Inc., 1957.
2. Tennessee Williams, *Sweet Bird of Youth.* New York, New Directions, 1959.
3. *The Open Door,* St. Leonard's House, Chicago, Illinois.
4. From a letter to a friend, written from Tamanrasset, August 15, 1916, published in *Jesus Caritas.* He restated this principle in a letter written on May 1, 1912: "One learns to love God by loving men."
5. Michel Quoist, quoted in *Jesus Caritas*, October, 1958.

CHAPTER V

1. Adlai Stevenson, in *Saturday Review,* February 7, 1959. © 1959, Adlai E. Stevenson.
2. Paul Bowles, in *Holiday*, April 1959.
3. Elizabeth Bowen, *The House in Paris.* New York, Alfred A. Knopf, Inc., 1936.
4. Simone de Beauvoir, *The Mandarins.* New York, World Publishing Co., 1957.
5. James Agee, *A Death in the Family.* New York, McDowell, Obolensky Inc., 1957.

CHAPTER VI

1. Consuelo Vanderbilt Balsan, *The Glitter and the Gold.* New York, Harper & Brothers, 1952.

CHAPTER VII

1. Martin Mayer, *Madison Avenue, U.S.A.* New York, Harper & Brothers, 1958.
2. William Lynch, S.J., *The Image Industries.* New York. Sheed & Ward, Inc., 1959.
3. New York, Doubleday & Co., 1957.
4. Michael Scott, *A Time to Speak.* New York, Doubleday & Co., Inc., 1958.

OTHER TITLES

in the

LIBRARY OF EPISCOPALIAN CLASSICS

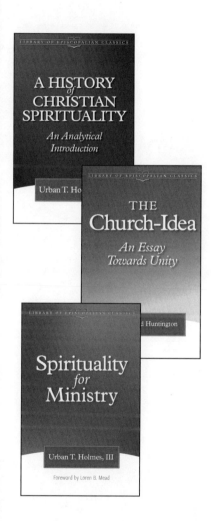

A HISTORY *of* CHRISTIAN SPIRITUALITY

Urban T. Holmes, III

176 pages, paperback
0-8192-1914-2

THE CHURCH-IDEA

An Essay Towards Unity

William Reed Huntington

192 pages, paperback
0-8192-1913-4

SPIRITUALITY *for* MINISTRY

Urban T. Holmes, III

208 pages, paperback
0-8192-1916-9
(TO BE PUBLISHED IN FALL 2002)

MOREHOUSE PUBLISHING